BEST

TRAIL RUNS

SEATTLE

ADAM W. CHASE | NANCY HOBBS

FALCONGUIDES®

GUILFORD, CONNECTICUT

FALCONGUIDES®

An imprint of Globe Pequot

Falcon and FalconGuides are registered trademarks and Make Adventure Your Story is a trademark of Rowman & Littlefield.

Distributed by NATIONAL BOOK NETWORK
Copyright © 2017 Rowman & Littlefield

Maps: Melissa Baker © 2017 Rowman & Littlefield

British Library Cataloguing in Publication Information available

Library of Congress Cataloging-in-Publication Data available

ISBN 978-1-4930-2516-9 (paperback)
ISBN 978-1-4930-2517-6 (e-book)

∞™ The paper used in this publication meets the minimum requirements of American National Standard for Information Sciences—Permanence of Paper for Printed Library Materials, ANSI/NISO Z39.48-1992.

Printed in the United States of America

INTRODUCTION

SEATTLE HAS LONG BEEN AN EPICENTER FOR TRAIL RUN-NING. Maybe that is because the lush, verdant landscapes give runners the feeling of being ants in a terrarium, lulled by traveling over many a mile on soft ground through coniferous forests. That explains why there are already several well-written, thoroughly researched trail-running guides for the area and even more hiking guides for the same territory. And, really, what is the difference between a running and hiking trail? With that many resources already available to trail runners seeking enticing trails to explore, what distinguishes this guide?

We didn't undertake this project because we thought we could do a "better" job than those who have written others but, rather, because we thought we could bring new trails to light, and that our presentation of the trails we've selected is written from a different and up-to-date perspective. In fact, that is what prompted us to recruit our friend, the omnipresent Glenn Tachiyama, to join us in putting together this guide. Many of you have seen Glenn out on the trails, and there is a good chance that he's even photographed you. He knows well most of these trails, having run and captured photographs of almost every inch of Seattle's off-road terrain. Together with Glenn, it is our aim to provide you with fresh, new trails to accompany the traditional, sure-bet, can't-miss runs of the Seattle area.

Combined with Glenn's photography, we are excited about the authenticity and local grit you'll find in this guide.

It has been our objective, either through *The Ultimate Guide to Trail Running* or our roles with the American Trail Running Association (ATRA), to help hikers accelerate into trail runners, assist road runners in converting and adapting to trails, and provide direction for current trail runners to become stronger, more agile, and efficient. While we've been able to tackle the "how" in past work, this book allows us to take on the "where."

People who don't like precipitation shouldn't live here, especially if they want to sport a year-round tan. Whether it is chicken or egg is a good question, but Seattle is home to REI and other top-notch gear companies, adding emphasis to the saying "there's no such thing as bad weather, just bad gear (or a bad attitude)." Knowing your route and not being lost are great attitude enhancers, so while we can't help you with the weather, we can provide some guidance on gear, training, nutrition, and preparedness.

Best Trail Runs Seattle addresses running on wet ground, through water and mud, and the related concerns of exposure, traction, and other safety factors. The guide also discusses gear choices for the various weather conditions you are likely to face on the trails we've included. Given our positions with the American Trail Running Association, we've also incorporated a discussion of when not to run on muddy trails and environmental concerns that are unique to Seattle trail running.

DIFFICULTY RATINGS

Being that many trail runners are also Alpine skiers who understand the meaning of easy/green, intermediate (moderate)/blue, and difficult/black for rating the difficulty of a run, we chose to go with that for the trails in this book. We acknowledge the subjective nature of this, noting that one

GEAR
Normally, being prepared for the trail doesn't require much, and, in fact, taking too much gear soon takes away from the experience, as you are bogged down or distracted, not to mention you are likely heavy, slow, and overheating. While this guide features rather in-depth discussions of different trail-running equipment, from shoes to headwear, we also emphasize what you don't need. Other than the essentials of shoes, socks, shorts, water-shielding top, and possibly warmer apparel, sunglasses, hydration, and a watch, you don't need much—and that is one of the allures of trail running. Less is more.

person's hard is another's easy, but we did want to guide readers with some sense of relative ease or difficulty so that they may plan accordingly.

CELL PHONE COVERAGE

We also deemed it helpful to readers to know if a trail has cell phone coverage. This is merely for safety purposes. We urge trail runners to use proper etiquette and to refrain from using phones, except in cases of emergency or to take pictures of the beautiful scenery through which these trails run.

Getting Started

Whereas road running is a more straightforward, linear function, trail training is multidimensional because it blends lateral motion with forward movement. To adapt your training routine to accommodate varying terrain inherent in trails, you will need to focus on strengthening your stabilizing muscles and balance. Similarly, because you will surely encounter hills—both steep climbs and steady climbs—as a trail runner, you should consider the benefits of including training workouts that focus on strength, such as running hill repeats of varying intervals and distance. If you want to become a faster and fitter trail runner, you should consider increasing your speed through repeats, improving your fitness by running intervals and speed drills, and, finally, you may want to hit the weight room and incorporate a stretching regime.

It is not very easy to find a flat trail in Seattle. True, the flat trail does exist, but given its relative rarity, Puget Sound trail runners become quickly and painfully aware of the importance and benefits of hill training.

Pacing or economy of effort are probably the most important aspects of effective hill running. Much to their regret, novice trail runners are frequently less inclined (no pun intended) to use appropriate pacing on hills. As a result, they face the consequences of sputtering out with burning calves, huffing lungs, and possibly even nausea long before reaching the summit. Those new to hilly trails also tend to use improper form when descending and, accordingly, suffer from aching quadriceps and knee joints.

Running hills efficiently is a skill acquired through a process of fine-tuning and lots of practice, accounting for differences in body type, strength, weaknesses, agility, fitness, and aversion to risk. Armed with proper technique, a trail runner is prepared to take on hills—or mountains, for that matter—with alacrity instead of dread.

Whether you should attack with speed or power hike a hill or steep ascent is a complex decision that depends on the length of the climb, the trail surface, your level of fatigue, the altitude, the distance of the run, at what point in the run you encounter the hill, and whether you are training or racing. Efficient power hiking is often faster than running, especially in longer runs, when the footing is difficult, or at high altitude. It can be very rewarding to hike past someone who is trying to run up a hill and know that you are expending far less effort while you move at a faster pace. Conversely, it is quite demoralizing to be passed by a hiker while you struggle to run up a steep incline.

Two crucial elements of being a strong hill runner are tempo and confidence. A runner who is able to maintain tempo, cadence, or rhythm ascending and descending a hill will be more efficient and generally faster on hills than a runner who tries to muscle up and down the same slope in fits and starts. Two secrets to maintaining your tempo on a hill is the discipline and ability to adjust stride length.

Observing the fastest and most efficient climbers, both human and animal, it is easy to note their sustained turnover with a shortened stride on the climb. Even speedy mountain types go slower uphill and faster downhill, but the cadence of their legs hardly changes, regardless of the grade, the only difference being stride length. Just as you shift into lower gear when you bicycle up a hill, you need to shift gears as a runner by shortening your stride length.

A short stride on both the ascent and descent works very well on trails that are particularly rugged with difficult footing. By using many little steps, you are able to make quick adjustments to correct your footing on the fly. That allows you the most sure-footed landing for better traction and control. The ability to alter your path increases both your real and perceived control, which leads to a greater confidence, especially on descents. A heightened level of confidence on hills leads to a "heads-up" running style.

Proper form and confidence on hills increases a runner's enjoyment of inclines and declines and, at the same time, decreases the chances of injury.

SAFETY

With minimalism being de rigueur, Seattle trail runners should be aware that the trails we've selected tend to be relatively safe, so you needn't run with weapons. A whistle is probably more effective than any gun, knife, or can of pepper spray. You should assess weather trends from the trailhead and leave all that you don't need behind in your vehicle, locking it safely in your trunk rather than leaving it in plain view because, unfortunately, Puget Sound trailheads have been targets for thieves.

With more confidence, you will be able to relax and run with a lighter, more flowing form that is more efficient and less painful. Knowing how to confront hills will keep you coming back for more, and because training on hills, whether on long, sustained ascents or shorter hill repeats, presents a superb opportunity for running-specific strength training, you will become a stronger and more confident runner overall.

Trail Training

Compared with road running, trail running requires a more balanced and comprehensive approach, incorporating the whole body. Trail runners must be prepared to handle varying terrain, conditions, steep inclines and declines, and other challenges not found on the road. Fortunately, one thing trail runners don't need to train for is dealing with motorized vehicles.

Although many of the following training techniques apply to road running, it is also necessary to perform them on trails if your goal is to become a better, more accomplished trail runner. Yes, you may become a faster road runner by doing speed work on the track; but that speed does not always transfer to trails, where you will be forced to use a different stride, constantly adjust your tempo for frequent gear changes, and maintain control while altering your body position to stay upright.

DISTANCE TRAINING

If your goal is to run or race a certain distance, then training for that distance will be a mandatory building block in your trail training regimen. Incorporating long runs into weekly training will help your body adjust physiologically to the increased impact-loading stress by generating more bone calcium deposits and by building more and stronger leg muscles and connective tissue. Building up weekly mileage improves your aerobic capacity to generate a base upon which you can mix speed and strength-training runs into your schedule.

Long training runs enable your body to cope with high mileage by breaking down fats for fuel and becoming more biomechanically efficient. Psychologically, long runs teach you to cope with and understand fatigue. During lengthy training runs, runners frequently experience what can become an emotional roller coaster. It is useful to become familiar with how you respond under such circumstances, especially if you are training for a longer distance trail race. Long runs also help build confidence as a measure of progress. And, perhaps best, these runs become adventures into unchartered territory, allowing you to explore new stretches of trails and see new sites.

Some simple advice for those converting from roads to trails—especially for those who keep a log to record time, distance, and pace—is to forget about training distance or, if you know the distance of a trail, leave your watch behind when you go for a training run. Since trail running is invariably slower than road running, you will only get frustrated if you make the common mistake of comparing your trail pace with your road or track pace.

A prime reason for running trails is to escape tedious calculations, so free yourself from distance and time constraints and just run and enjoy, particularly during your initial exposure to trail running. Tap into the wonderful feeling of breezing by brush and trees as you flow up and down hills and maneuver sharp corners with skill and agility. You can always fret about your pace as you develop your trail skills and speed.

If you base your trail-running training on the premise that long runs are primarily a function of time rather than ground covered, you should keep training runs close to the amount of time you think it will take to run your target distance. For example, if you are training to complete a 5.0-mile trail run in the near future, you might set your training run for 45 minutes. If, however, you are training for a trail marathon or ultramarathon, you probably want to keep your distance training to somewhat less than the time it will take you to complete the race distance. To get to that point, you may want to set aside between one day every two weeks to two days a week for long runs, depending on your goal, experience, fitness background, and resistance to injury.

Trail runners usually dedicate one day of the week for a considerably longer training run, although some prefer to run two relatively long days back-to-back, especially on weekends, when their schedules are more accommodating. This latter training method, known as a "brick workout," is common among ultramarathoners who must condition their bodies to perform while tired and stressed. Newer runners should not try brick workouts until they are both comfortable with trails and are confident that their bodies will be able to withstand two days of long runs without breaking down or suffering an injury.

Because the forgiving surface of trails, especially those in the Seattle area, may allow a person to run relatively injury-free, newer trail runners are often lulled into building up their distance base with long runs too rapidly. Whether performed on road or trail, distance running takes its toll on the body, and too quick an increase in distance often leads to injury, burnout, or leaving yourself prone to illness due to a compromised immune system. Depending on age, experience with endurance athletics in general, and your running history, it is better to increase your mileage or hours by no more than 5 to 10 percent per week.

Even if you increase your mileage base gradually, do not forfeit quality for quantity. Many runners succumb to the unhealthy game of comparing weekly mileages with either their previous weeks or with those of other runners. Junk miles are just that. Depending on your objectives, it is usually better to run fewer miles with fresher legs and at a more intense pace than to slog through miles merely to rack them up in your logbook.

One way to check the quality of your miles is to wear a heart rate monitor and couple the distance of your runs with the goal of staying within your training zone at a steady pace. If you find your heart rate consistently rising above or falling below that target rate as you tack on the miles, that is a sign you are overtraining; and it is unlikely you will derive much benefit from those miles unless you are training for ultradistance.

SPEED TRAINING

For some trail runners, just being out on the trails and communing with nature is enough. They don't care about their pace. Others want to increase their speed. Building up your distance base should help increase your running speed, but it only helps to a certain extent. To really pick it up and break through the barrier of your training pace, you should run fast. Running at a faster pace helps improve both cardiovascular fitness and biomechanical efficiency.

This discussion, however, is aimed at those who find it more exhilarating to push their limits, who enjoy the feeling of rushing along a wooded path, and who appreciate the fitness improvements that result from challenging themselves.

Beyond velocity, speed training—whether through intervals, repeats, tempo runs, fartleks, or other means—has positive physiological effects. Pushing the pace forces muscles and energy systems to adapt to the more strenuous effort. The body does this by improving the flow of blood to muscles, increasing the number of capillaries in muscle fiber, stimulating your muscles to increase their myoglobin and mitochondria content, and raising aerobic enzyme activity to allow muscles to produce more energy aerobically.

Running fast also provides a mental edge, because psychologically—if you are familiar with the stress and burning sensation known to many as "pain and suffering" that accompany running at a faster-than-normal pace during training—you will be able to draw from that experience and dig deeper into your reserves when needed during a race. Speed training on trails also forces you to push your comfort level with respect to the risk of falling or otherwise losing control on difficult terrain. Pushing the envelope helps establish a sense of confidence that is crucial to running difficult sections, especially descents, at speed.

Breaking away from the daily training pace and pushing oneself shakes up the routine and rejuvenates muscular, energy, and cardiovascular systems so that one may reprogram for a faster pace with more rapid leg speed and foot turnover. Running at a quicker pace than normal helps to realign running form and teaches respect for different speeds.

However, because speed training is an advanced form of training, it should not be introduced into one's routine before establishing a consistent training base. Beginning trail runners should start by becoming comfortable with running on trails before they endeavor to run those trails fast. Speed training stresses the body so it may be wise to do your faster workouts on tamer trails with dependable footing, dirt roads, or even a track or road.

INTERVALS

Although interval training improves leg speed, its primary goal is cardiovascular—to optimize lactate threshold. As an anaerobic training tool, intervals are designed to increase a runner's ability to maintain a fast pace for a longer period of time. Without an improvement in lactate threshold, the runner will be unable to run or race a substantial distance at a faster pace than the rate at which the body can comfortably use oxygen, thereby causing lactate to form in the bloodstream. Intervals help to raise the level at which the body begins the lactate production process so that the runner is able to run faster and longer without feeling muscles burn or cramp. Upon developing a substantial training base of endurance, speed intervals allow acceleration of pace and an increase in overall running fitness.

Intervals are usually measured in terms of time rather than distance, especially if run on hilly or rugged trails. During the "on" or hard-effort segments of interval training, trail runners should work hard enough to go anaerobic (i.e., faster than your lactate or anaerobic threshold so that the body goes into oxygen debt). During the "off" or recovery segments, you are allowed to repay some of the oxygen debt, but not all of it. The rest period should be sufficiently short so that you are "on" again before full recovery.

An interval workout may be a series of equal on-and-off interval and recovery periods or a mix of different length intervals and recoveries. For example, a trail runner might run six intervals of four minutes each, interspersed with three-minute recoveries. Alternatively, the interval session might mix it up with five-, four-, three-, two-, three-, four-, and five-minute intervals, each separated by a three-minute recovery.

Intervals may be as long as six minutes and as short as thirty seconds. Run intervals at a pace that is a bit faster than lactate threshold, which is usually equivalent to the pace run when racing a distance from 2 miles to 5 kilometers in length. The interval pace should be uncomfortable, but not excruciating; although not a sprint, you should feel you are running fast.

Run longer intervals if training for longer distances and shorter intervals if speed is the goal. The off (recovery) period between intervals is an active rest that ranges between jogging and moderate running. Recovery time should be a little shorter than the time of the interval preceding it. In addition to recoveries between the intervals, any interval workout should integrate a substantial warm-up before and cooldown after running.

HILL REPEATS AND REPETITION WORKOUTS

"Repeats" resemble intervals, except that leg speed and strength are emphasized more than lactate threshold (although repetition workouts have some beneficial lactate threshold effects). Put another way, repeat workouts are designed for biomechanical and physiological improvement more than for cardiovascular benefits. Hill repeats are intended to hone your climbing skills and generally make for a stronger runner by taxing the muscular system with anaerobic intervals.

Repeats are run at or faster than the lactate threshold pace, and each interval is shorter in length than in a standard interval workout. Typically, repeats last two minutes or less; and because repeats are more intense than intervals, the recovery period is longer. Since the focus is muscle strength improvement rather than fitness, the active rest between repeats should be long enough to recharge and prepare for the next repeat at or above lactate threshold. In short, if you run a two-minute repeat and need three minutes to recover, take the full three minutes. You want to recover enough to make each repeat interval sufficiently intense to realize the full benefits of the exercise.

Run each interval at a pace that you can maintain through the entire repeat workout. Don't push so hard during early repeats that you are unable to finish the rest of the workout. Hill repeats provide a great strength and lactate threshold workout with minimal stress to the body, because you push hard to go anaerobic while climbing, but then rest as you slowly jog or walk to the bottom of the hill. Because of the reduced stress, you can throw hill repeats into your training schedule on a weekly basis without jeopardizing the health of your connective tissue.

TEMPO RUNS

Imagine a spectrum with repeats that focus on biomechanics and muscular strength buildup at one end, intervals that focus on a combination of lactate threshold and biomechanics in the middle, and tempo runs at the other end, which emphasize lactate threshold or cardiovascular fitness.

Repeats   **Intervals**   **Tempo Runs**

|———————————————————————————————————————|

Biomechanics/Strength   **Cardio/Lactate Threshold**

Tempo runs are sustained efforts at an even pace, usually lasting 20 to 40 minutes; although those training for longer distances may do tempo runs that stretch to 90 minutes. The pace should be a lactate threshold pace, which is faster than the pace at which you are able to maintain a conversation, but not faster than one that forces you to exceed 90 percent of maximum heart rate. The pace could be maintained for about an hour, if racing. Since the goal of tempo training is to maintain a steady pace with consistent leg turnover, run tempos on a trail or dirt road that is relatively flat with good footing.

Tempo runs should include a warm-up and cooldown, both at a comfortable pace. If the tempo workout involves training partners, be careful to not turn the session into a race or time trial. To prevent that from occurring, wear a heart rate monitor and set it to sound an alarm if the heart rate rises above lactate threshold rate. Because tempo runs are physiological workouts, the goal is to run at a certain effort rather than to cover a certain distance. Depending on terrain, weather, or how rested you are beginning a tempo run, the pace may vary, but the body should nevertheless be working at threshold level throughout the workout.

Because considerable concentration and focus are required to maintain a steady lactate threshold pace for twenty minutes or longer, runners frequently find themselves a bit tired, both physically and mentally, the next day or two after a tempo workout. If that is the case, take a day of active rest or work a recovery run into your schedule. It may even be advisable to take the next day off to rest up and maintain trail-running vigor.

FARTLEKS

Fartlek is Swedish for "speed play." Scandinavians, known for their trail-running prowess and long history in the sport, pioneered the art of running fast on trails. Fartleks are creative workouts that weave a variety of paces into the same run. Although fartleks can be performed solo, they are often run as a group, in single file with the leader setting the pace—sometimes sprinting, sometimes jogging, sometimes walking, at other times simply running. Because the pace of a fartlek often varies with the terrain, these invigorating workouts are most successful if run on trails that offer a mix of short and long hills and plenty of turns and obstacles.

Fartleks offer a fun alternative to more standardized, timed speed workouts. Because they lack any regimented order, fartleks can reinject zip into a training routine that has grown boring or introduce some excitement when running feels lethargic. The pacesetter can rotate, and faster runners may loop back to pick up stragglers to keep the fartlek group intact.

To capture some benefits of a fartlek when running alone, throw in some surges to get some speed training. Surges are short blasts of speed worked into a training run to accentuate a transition in the trail, such as near the top of a hill or at the bottom of a hill when beginning a climb.

Another way to mix training with a little speed is to integrate striders or accelerations into the routine. An excellent time to insert some striders or accelerations is at the end of a trail run, just before the cooldown. Striders and accelerations are usually performed on flat, soft surfaces such as grassy parks, playing fields, or dirt roads. If striders or accelerations are run on grass or sand, try removing shoes so as to work on the muscle tone of lower legs and feet while feeling light and free. Strider and acceleration distances should range between 50 and 100 meters, allowing for an additional 10 meters to get started and 20 to 30 meters to slow down.

A strider is usually run at a fast running pace, just under or even finishing with a sprint. Place emphasis on high knee lifts and getting a full kick off each step so as to cover as much ground as possible without overstriding. When striding, think of sprinters warming up on a track, swinging arms and lifting knees in an accentuated manner. Accelerations resemble striders, but begin more slowly and end in a full sprint.

"OFF-TRAIL" SPEED TRAINING

Although the goal of speed training is to improve physiology, the cardiovascular system, biomechanics, the muscular system, and mental strength, it is not necessary to do all speed training on trails. In fact, it is more effective to perform some speed-training sessions on the track, dirt roads, or even paved roads. Depending on where you live and the types of trails to which you have access, it may be a lot easier to do speed training off the trails, reserving the trip to trails for longer runs.

Road and track are better suited for certain types of speed training. Tempo runs, where the focus is on a steady pace, and repeats, where the emphasis is on leg turnover, should be performed on flatter, more dependable surfaces. Roads or tracks are certainly easier than the trail for these types of workouts, especially if trails are icy or muddy.

Track sessions tend to be highly efficient. Perhaps it is the lane lines or the bends of the turns, but something about running on a track creates a feeling of running fast. That feeling may well convert to actual speed, which means a more effective speed session. Tracks are also a helpful option because they are measured for convenient pacing. If you want to do repeats or intervals and maintain a set pace, going to the track is an efficient alternative to the trail.

In addition to selecting the appropriate speed workout and venue for the session, also take the weather into consideration. If it is snowy, icy, muddy, or particularly windy, it may not be possible to get a good speed workout outside. Depending on training needs and personal preferences, train inside and run a set of repeats or intervals on the treadmill or work on leg turnover with some spinning. However, many trail runners are adamantly opposed to such mechanical alternatives and insist on running outside, regardless of the weather. That is fine and well, but they then must be willing to either forego speed-training sessions when the weather is particularly nasty or attempt to do them in unfavorable conditions.

seattle proper

SAINT EDWARD STATE PARK

PART OF THE WASHINGTON STATE PARK SYSTEM, THIS 316-ACRE PARK offers about 6 miles of trails, many of which are forested. You will also find sections through open meadows, as well as a singletrack trail along the Lake Washington beachfront. There are several points from which to access the trail system in the park, as well as from nearby Bastyr University. There are flat runs and more challenging ascending and descending runs (upward of 42 percent), afforded by the North and South Trails that lead to the lake. The trails are not very well marked beyond a sign at each trailhead. Because of that and the many junctions you'll come across without markings, it may be best to copy the trail map or take a picture of it and carry it with you for reference as you follow the route.

SAINT EDWARD STATE PARK

THE RUN DOWN

START: At the trailhead across from Bastyr University; elevation 432 feet

OVERALL DISTANCE: 2.7-mile loop

APPROXIMATE RUNNING TIME: 40 minutes

DIFFICULTY: Blue (due to climbing)

ELEVATION GAIN: 404 feet

BEST SEASON TO RUN: Year-round

DOG FRIENDLY: Leashed dogs permitted

PARKING: A day fee is charged in the State Park, or purchase an annual WA Discovery Pass

OTHER USERS: Mountain bikers on designated trails; no equestrians

CELL PHONE COVERAGE: Good

MORE INFORMATION: http://parks.state.wa.us/577/Saint-Edward

SAINT EDWARD STATE PARK

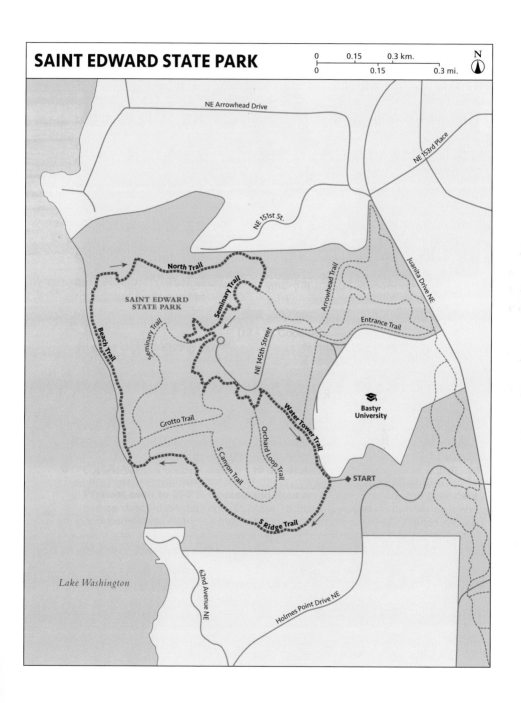

0   0.15   0.3 km.

0   0.15   0.3 mi.

N

NE Arrowhead Drive

NE 153rd Place

NE 151st St.

North Trail

Juanita Drive NE

Seminary Trail

SAINT EDWARD
STATE PARK

Arrowhead Trail

Beach Trail

Seminary Trail

Entrance Trail

NE 145th Street

Grotto Trail

Water Tower Trail

Bastyr
University

Orchard Loop Trail

S Canyon Trail

START

S Ridge Trail

Lake Washington

62nd Avenue NE

Holmes Point Drive NE

Saint Edward State Park
PHOTO BY NANCY HOBBS

FINDING THE TRAILHEAD

Heading west from the 405 on Highway 522, turn left on 68th Avenue NE. Continue to Juanita Drive NE, turn right on 145th Street and head uphill to the parking lot at Bastyr University. To access the trails directly in Saint Edward Park, follow 145th Street to the right at the intersection below the university.

Although this route can be accessed in numerous spots, the start point of this clockwise loop is on the Plateau Trail across the road from Bastyr University. No restrooms are at the trailhead, but there are restrooms in the park.

RUN DESCRIPTION

Mostly singletrack, with a few short sections of steps on the South Ridge and North Trails to assist with the ascending and descending, this is a good route for hill intervals if training for races with steep ascents. There are a few short, paved sections on this route near the Saint Edward Seminary and adjacent buildings (this area was once a Catholic seminary) and a short section on the Perimeter Trail that connects with the Watertower Trail to complete the loop. Taking a dip in Lake Washington may be an enjoyable addition to training on a hot day.

CARKEEK PARK

WITH VIEWS OF THE PUGET SOUND AND OLYMPIC MOUNTAINS, THIS outstanding city park venue encompasses 220 acres with 6 miles of trails, most of which are singletrack or wider, hard-packed gravel paths. Some of the trails are within the forest, while others are in more open areas and meadows. In addition to natural obstacles, such as rocks and tree roots, runners will confront steps and footbridges on many of the trails. You will also find log benches convenient for a meditative moment during your excursions in Carkeek Park. There are numerous access points to the trails, some in surrounding neighborhoods, others within the park itself. The boundaries and course markings are indicated at most junctions, but it is a good idea (as is the theme in this guide) to carry a map to better navigate the intended route.

Runners should be wary of the fact that this is a very busy area because, like many of the city and state park venues, Carkeek Park is an epicenter of myriad activities. This is a particularly family-friendly venue, with the play areas and picnic spots as well as some ADA-compatible, accessible terrain for people of all ages and abilities. After running the trails, practice some ascending on the road (or adjacent sidewalk) starting at NW Carkeek Park Road to NW 116th Street and beyond.

CARKEEK PARK 2.4-MILE

THE RUN DOWN

START: At the trailhead in the westernmost parking lot; elevation 33 feet

OVERALL DISTANCE: 2.4 miles out and back with a keyhole route

APPROXIMATE RUNNING TIME: 35 minutes

DIFFICULTY: Blue

ELEVATION GAIN: 422 feet

BEST SEASON TO RUN: Year-round, but can have muddy spots

DOG FRIENDLY: Leashed dogs permitted

PARKING: Free

OTHER USERS: Mountain bikers on designated trails and roads

CELL PHONE COVERAGE: Good

MORE INFORMATION: www .seattle.gov/parks/trails_ detail.asp?id=240

FINDING THE TRAILHEAD

From Seattle, take I-5 North to NW 85th Street. Turn right on 3rd Avenue NW, then left on NW 110th Street, which becomes NW Carkeek Park Road. Park at the westernmost lot by Puget Sound and the nearby railroad tracks, and head west down the steps. Turn left on the South Ridge Trail to run in a counterclockwise direction with a short out-and-back section outside the park boundary—just one of the many neighborhood access points.

FLORA AND FAUNA

Weapons to ward off the unlikely possibility of animal encounters are an unnecessary encumbrance on Seattle trails unless you are running in the remotest areas. High user traffic tends to cause animals such as coyotes, cougars, and bears to take refuge. An occasional rattlesnake, mostly seen at lower elevations, may be cause for some sidestepping on the trail. Bugs and pesky gnats are virtually nonexistent. The only annoying plants are those with burrs and the occasional stinging nettle.

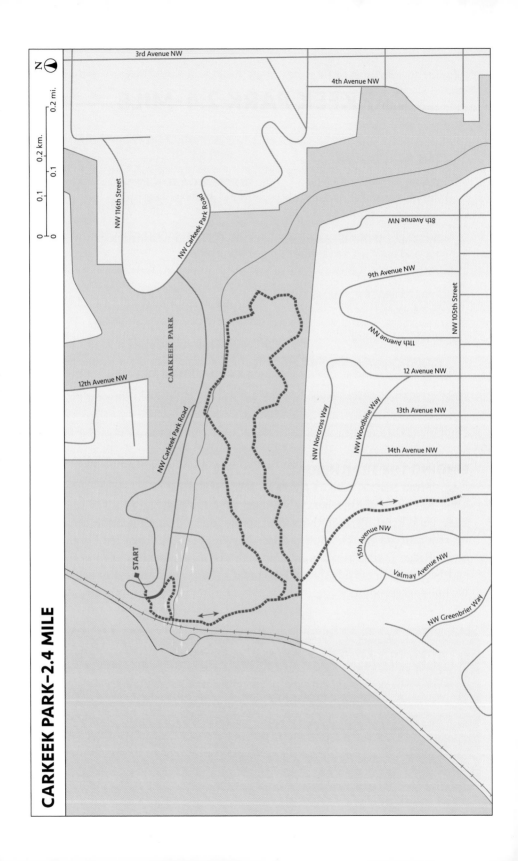

CARKEEK PARK–2.4 MILE

N

0   0.1   0.2 km.

0   0.1   0.2 mi.

3rd Avenue NW

4th Avenue NW

NW 116th Street

NW Carkeek Park Road

8th Avenue NW

CARKEEK PARK

9th Avenue NW

NW 105th Street

11th Avenue NW

12th Avenue NW

12 Avenue NW

NW Norcross Way

13th Avenue NW

NW Woodbine Way

14th Avenue NW

NW Carkeek Park Road

START

15th Avenue NW

Valmay Avenue NW

NW Greenbrier Way

Carkeet Park.
PHOTO BY NANCY HOBBS

RUN DESCRIPTION

The relatively smooth running surface has steps at various intervals on climbs and/or descents depending on the direction in which the route is run. Some junctions are not marked, and some of the spur trails are not named on the park map. Even so, it is a fairly easy route to follow—aided, of course, by carrying a map from this book or taking a picture of the one at the trailhead. Well-maintained plank boardwalk bridges cross Pipers Creek at two spots along the route. Even though the majority of the trails are fairly smooth, there are some exposed roots and rocks, just to give you a true trail-running experience. Much of the trail is under a forested canopy.

CARKEEK PARK LOOP WITH A SHORT OUT-AND-BACK SECTION

THE RUN DOWN

START: At the trailhead in the westernmost parking lot; elevation 52 feet

OVERALL DISTANCE: 0.7 mile (with additional trail connections possible)

APPROXIMATE RUNNING TIME: 10 minutes

DIFFICULTY: Blue

ELEVATION GAIN: 159 feet

BEST SEASON TO RUN: Year-round

DOG FRIENDLY: Leashed dogs permitted

PARKING: Free

OTHER USERS: None

CELL PHONE COVERAGE: Good

MORE INFORMATION: www .seattle.gov/parks/trails_ detail.asp?id=240

Carkeet Park.
PHOTO BY NANCY HOBBS

CARKEEK PARK–
SHORT OUT-AND-BACK

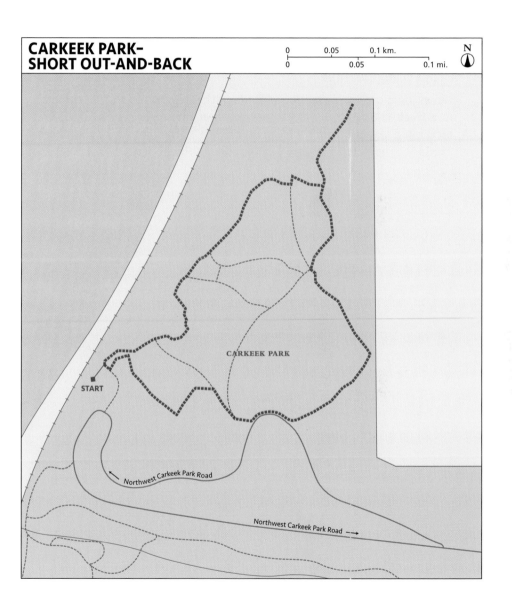

FINDING THE TRAILHEAD

 This trailhead is in the westernmost section of the park, on the north side, just beyond the picnic tables.

RUN DESCRIPTION

Start on an uphill to enjoy the trails on the north side of the park, aptly named the North Bluff Trail and North Traverse Trail, with some additional short unnamed junctions. Climb up the steps to run this short loop in a clockwise direction. Continue uphill on the singletrack to an open meadow. Enjoy the view and head back down on the Grand Fir Trail, connecting to the North Traverse Trail to close the loop.

SEWARD PARK

THIS 300-ACRE CITY PARK HAS ALMOST 6 MILES OF TRAILS, BOTH RUGGED and groomed. As a landmass, the park juts out as a peninsula into Lake Washington. Several parking lots are located within the park that serve as launch points for easy, flat runs. In addition to a perimeter loop on the road, singletrack and wider pathways wind through the inner section of the park, in and out of the forest. The park gets congested on the weekends and in the summer. Early morning is a great time to enjoy solitude on the trails, but wait until the park opens at 6 a.m.

PERIMETER TRAIL

THE RUN DOWN

START: On the road at the Pottery building; elevation 26 feet

OVERALL DISTANCE: 2.5 miles

APPROXIMATE RUNNING TIME: 25 minutes

DIFFICULTY: Green

ELEVATION GAIN: None

BEST SEASON TO RUN: Year-round

DOG FRIENDLY: Leashed dogs permitted

PARKING: Free

OTHER USERS: Cyclists

CELL PHONE COVERAGE: Good

MORE INFORMATION: www.seattle.gov/Parks/environment/seward.htm

FINDING THE TRAILHEAD

From Seattle, take I-5 South to S. Albro Place, exit 161. Turn left on S. Graham Street, and follow to 42nd Avenue South. Turn left and follow to S. Orca Street. Turn right and park in the lot located just east of Lake Washington Street South within the confines of the park. Start on the road at the Pottery building.

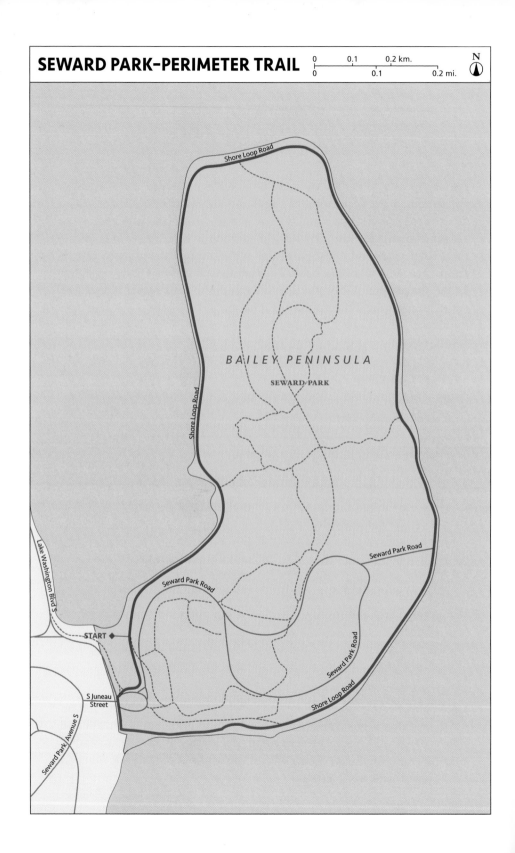

SEWARD PARK-PERIMETER TRAIL

0   0.1   0.2 km.

0   0.1   0.2 mi.

N

Shore Loop Road

BAILEY PENINSULA

SEWARD PARK

Shore Loop Road

Seward Park Road

Lake Washington Blvd S

Seward Park Road

Seward Park Road

START

S Juneau Street

Shore Loop Road

Seward Park Avenue S

Seward Park.
PHOTO BY NANCY HOBBS

RUN DESCRIPTION

Follow the road in a clockwise direction. For a softer surface, take the singletrack pathway running adjacent to the road. Each 0.5 mile is marked with a concrete signpost, so this makes for excellent tempo training with measured efforts.

INNER TRAIL

THE RUN DOWN

START: On the road at the Pottery building; elevation 0 feet

OVERALL DISTANCE: 1.7-mile larger outer loop with smaller inner loop

APPROXIMATE RUNNING TIME: 20 minutes

DIFFICULTY: Green

ELEVATION GAIN: 120 feet

BEST SEASON TO RUN: Year-round

DOG FRIENDLY: Leashed dogs permitted

PARKING: Free

OTHER USERS: Foot traffic only on the trails; cyclists on the road

CELL PHONE COVERAGE: Good

MORE INFORMATION: www.seattle.gov/Parks/environment/seward.htm

FINDING THE TRAILHEAD

Park in the lot located just east of Lake Washington Street South within the confines of the park. Start on the road at the Pottery building.

RUN DESCRIPTION

Follow the road in a clockwise direction for about 0.25 mile, then take the Andrews Bay Trail on the right side, heading uphill on steps to the inner trail system. Run on sections of the Sqebeqsed Trail in the forest, as well

WEATHER AS THE COACH

Many runners "let the weather be the coach," selecting their trail destinations based on whether it is wet and muddy or cold and icy. Forest runs are especially attractive as a cool respite from occasional hot and humid streaks. Occasional Pineapple Express storms can bring strong rain and wind, and it is the latter that may make the forest a dangerous place. Having a tree fall on you can really ruin your day.

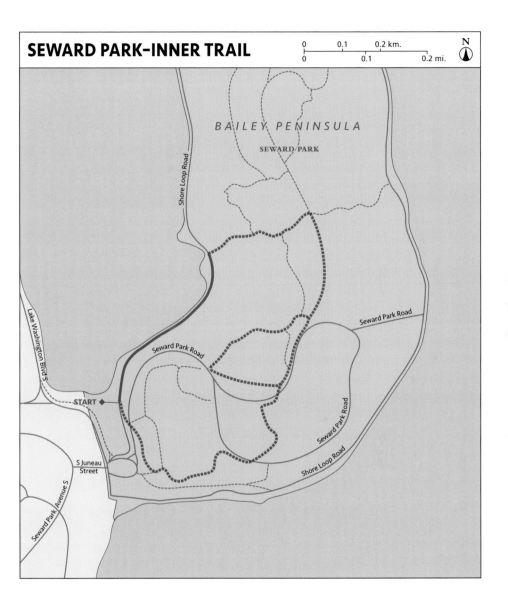

as the Lost Lake and Clark's Prairie Trail. There are also some sections through a grassy meadow by the amphitheater. The trails are very well marked and never far from the Seward Park Road, which travels through the park.

CROSS-TRAINING

TRAIL RUNNERS ARE OFTEN WELL-ROUNDED ATHLETES who enjoy a fine collection of outdoor endurance activities. With the changing seasons, trail runners are likely to supplement their recreational routines with Alpine and Nordic skiing; snowshoeing; kayaking; swimming; pool running; climbing; hiking; walking; martial arts; dance; horseback riding; skating; mountain, road, and stationary biking; and other pursuits. Engaging in other sports helps balance a trail runner's training regimen, develop supporting muscles, and condition the cardio system, and throws an element of excitement and vivaciousness into the mix. Because running is not necessarily a full-body sport, integrating other activities into training helps strengthen the trunk and upper body, which might otherwise grow weak from neglect.

Skills and strengths gained from cross-training easily translate to trail running. The limbering and strengthening of muscles that come from rock climbing, the lung capacity gained from Nordic skiing, high-altitude training from mountaineering, descending skills from mountain biking, the leg strength gained from snowshoeing, the muscular balance gained from swimming—all of these make for a better trail runner.

Cross-training also gives some perspective to trail running. Cross-training can be used as "active rest"; you can feel good about not running while pursuing another discipline or developing new skills that enhance the trail-running dimension. By becoming passionate about other athletic endeavors, a trail runner is more likely to take adequate time away from running when a recovery period is necessary to recuperate from an overuse injury or to avoid overuse. Knowing there are alternatives to running trails certainly helps during a time of injury, boredom, or burnout from running.

Cross-training is easily integrated into the trail-running routine by substituting a different discipline for a running session or two each week. These cross-training sessions should be of equivalent intensity as the running would have been, as measured by heart rate, effort, and time. For example, after a long trail run on Sunday, replace the normal 45-minute Monday recovery run with a 45-minute swim, bike, or Nordic ski session of equivalent effort.

Depending on your trail-running goals, cross-training should complement and supplement running, but not supplant it. Although cross-training is an excellent way to maintain fitness while giving running muscles some time off, cross-training should be thought of as active rest, in that it should not be so strenuous or depleting that you are too exhausted to pursue trail-running training. Exercise some caution when trying a new sport, because it is easy to strain muscles that are not trained for that specific activity. It is rather disappointing to spoil your trail-running training effort because of an injury resulting from a cross-training mishap.

RAVENNA PARK/ COWEN PARK

AT ONLY 49 ACRES, THIS PARK SYSTEM IS NOT LARGE. BUT IT IS A HIDDEN GEM. The hard-packed gravel perimeter trails and sidewalks provide no indication that in the center of the park magnificent singletrack trails offer a very serene experience. The 4.5 miles of trails are in open meadows as well as in the forest and, at points, cross over Ravenna Creek on planked footbridges. Capitalizing on the urban nature of the park, there are access points throughout the park to adjacent neighborhoods as well as flights of stairs to take you from the upper trails to those found running along the creek bed.

RAVENNA PARK/COWEN PARK

THE RUN DOWN

START: Gravel path at the Ravenna Ave. NE parking lot; elevation 131 feet

OVERALL DISTANCE: 1.7 miles of interconnected loops

APPROXIMATE RUNNING TIME: 25 minutes

DIFFICULTY: Green

ELEVATION GAIN: 171 feet

BEST SEASON TO RUN: Year-round

DOG FRIENDLY: Leashed dogs permitted

PARKING: Free

OTHER USERS: Mountain bikers

CELL PHONE COVERAGE: Good

MORE INFORMATION: www .seattle.gov/parks/trails_ detail.asp?id=391

RAVENNA PARK/COWEN PARK

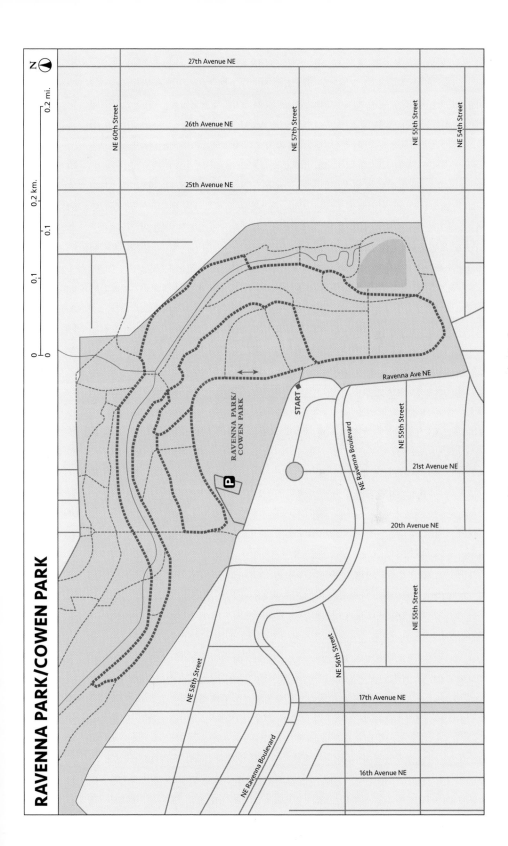

27th Avenue NE

NE 60th Street

26th Avenue NE

NE 57th Street

NE 55th Street

NE 54th Street

25th Avenue NE

0.2 mi.

0.2 km.

0.1

0.1

0.1

0

0

N

Ravenna Ave NE

START

RAVENNA PARK/
COWEN PARK

P

NE Ravenna Boulevard

NE 55th Street

21st Avenue NE

20th Avenue NE

NE 55th Street

NE 58th Street

NE 56th Street

17th Avenue NE

NE Ravenna Boulevard

16th Avenue NE

Ravenna Park
PHOTO BY NANCY HOBBS

FINDING THE TRAILHEAD

Park at the small lot located just east of Ravenna Avenue NE. There is a wide, crushed gravel pathway just steps away from the parking lot, where the run begins.

RUN DESCRIPTION

Turn left on the pathway and continue slightly uphill toward an open meadow. To the right are restrooms and a trail marker leading to steps down to the forested pathway below. Turn left at the bottom of the steps and run adjacent to Ravenna Creek, then cross at one of the footbridges, returning on the other side of the creek. Make a wide loop on the outer perimeter of the park, including a section on the sidewalk, and return to the start point for a short loop, or continue on the trail to add mileage. You'll enjoy an urban adventure on a mixture of singletrack trail, wide pathways, steps, and footbridges crossing over the creek on this route.

For postrun drinks or snacks, stop by Seven Coffee Roasters and Market, 2007 NE Ravenna Boulevard; or at the nearby Herkimer Coffee, 5611 University Way NE; or at Vegan Haven, 5270 University Way NE.

SEATTLE PROPER

DISCOVERY PARK

CONVENIENTLY LOCATED WITHIN 1 MILE OF THE SEVEN HILLS RUNNING SHOP—a must-stop location for expert trail-running advice—this park is Seattle's largest at 534 acres. The nearly 12 miles of trails invite trail runners of all levels to make the short trip from downtown Seattle to this location on the shores of Puget Sound.

A true gem, this park has it all. There's not only a wide variety of terrain, but Discovery Park also offers climbs and descents up and down wooden steps, wildflowers in abundance in the spring and summer, and absolutely amazing views of Shilshole Bay to the north and Salmon Bay waterway to the east. Trails are very well signed and cross Discovery Park Boulevard at several places in the park. The shorter Wolf Tree Nature Trail is accessed via the north parking lot, and unlike the majority of the park's trails, does not allow dogs.

Discovery Park.
PHOTO BY NANCY HOBBS

DISCOVERY PARK TOUR

THE RUN DOWN

START: Trailhead on the north side of the Discovery Park Visitor Center; elevation 246 feet

OVERALL DISTANCE: 4.6-mile loop

APPROXIMATE RUNNING TIME: 50 minutes

DIFFICULTY: Blue

ELEVATION GAIN: 413 feet

BEST SEASON TO RUN: Year-round, but can be muddy in the forest on the singletrack

DOG FRIENDLY: Leashed pets permitted on trails, not permitted on the beach

PARKING: Free

OTHER USERS: Foot traffic only on the trails; bikes on paved trails only

CELL PHONE COVERAGE: Very good

MORE INFORMATION: www .seattle.gov/parks/trails_ detail.asp?id=310

FINDING THE TRAILHEAD

The Discovery Park Visitor Center is located at the entrance to the park, off Discovery Park Boulevard near West Government Way. The trailhead is on the north side of the parking lot, indicating several start points for the trails.

RUN DESCRIPTION

This route starts on the Loop Trail, includes the South Beach and North Beach Trails, and is described in a clockwise direction. It consists primarily

WEATHER ESSENTIALS

Seattle runners know to carry adequate rainwear and dress in layers because mistakes of the unprepared may result in uncomfortable, if not severe, lessons. Running with hydration may not be as obvious when there is abundant humidity, but for many of the longer routes we've included in this guide, you should bring fluids, especially if it is likely to take you longer than the projected time or if the day is a hot one.

DISCOVERY PARK

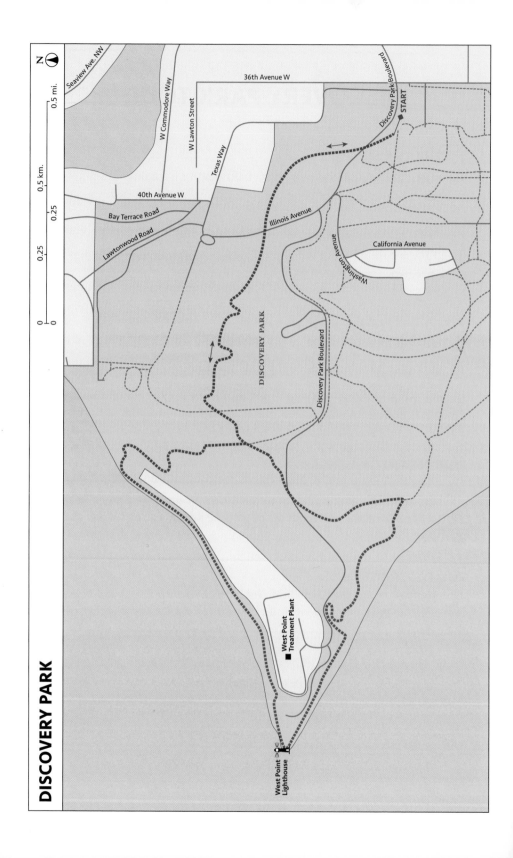

Discovery Park.
PHOTO BY NANCY HOBBS

of singletrack and wider pathways within the forest, with gentle, rolling terrain. The descent to the beach includes a variety of steps, some switchbacks, and great views. The flat section along the beach is about 1 mile in length and provides wonderful views of the shoreline as well as of the Cascade and Olympic mountain ranges.

After enjoying the flat respite, gear up for the climb, with grades between 10 and 30 percent. Although steep in spots, the total climb is less than 1 mile, then the route rejoins the Loop Trail for a rolling finish back to the start. This route features views of Puget Sound and Shilshole Bay, along with spectacular views of the Cascade and Olympic ranges. With a variety of wildflowers fully blooming in the springtime and seagulls riding the winds, this is a picturesque and serene spot.

After the run, be sure to stop in at the Seven Hills Running Shop, 3139 W Government Way. You can grab a coffee at Discovery Espresso at 3103 W Jameson Street or a burger and shake at 8oz Burger & Co. at 2409 Northwest Market Street.

LINCOLN PARK

THIS IS A VERY BUSY CITY PARK, primarily due to the variety of activities offered, such as a wading pool, a lap pool, picnic areas, and playing fields, in addition to the 4.6 miles of walking paths and 3.9 miles of bike trails, over 135 acres. The trails are numbered and named and fairly easy to follow, although junctions are not all marked.

LINCOLN PARK

THE RUN DOWN

START: At the trail map in the parking lot off Fauntleroy Way SW; elevation 130 feet

OVERALL DISTANCE: 1.9 miles

APPROXIMATE RUNNING TIME: 25 minutes

DIFFICULTY: Green

ELEVATION GAIN: 159 feet

BEST SEASON TO RUN: Year-round

DOG FRIENDLY: Leashed dogs permitted

PARKING: Free (but crowded)

OTHER USERS: Bikes on beachfront and designated trails

CELL PHONE COVERAGE: Good

MORE INFORMATION: www .seattle.gov/parks/park_detail .asp?ID=460

FINDING THE TRAILHEAD

From Seattle, head south on 99 and cross over the West Seattle bridge to Fauntleroy SW. Start at the parking lot off Fauntleroy Way SW, between SW Monroe and SW Rose Street by the large trail map.

RUN DESCRIPTION

Head north (right) at the trail sign and run a clockwise route, starting on a wide crushed gravel pathway. Continue past the wading pool and loop

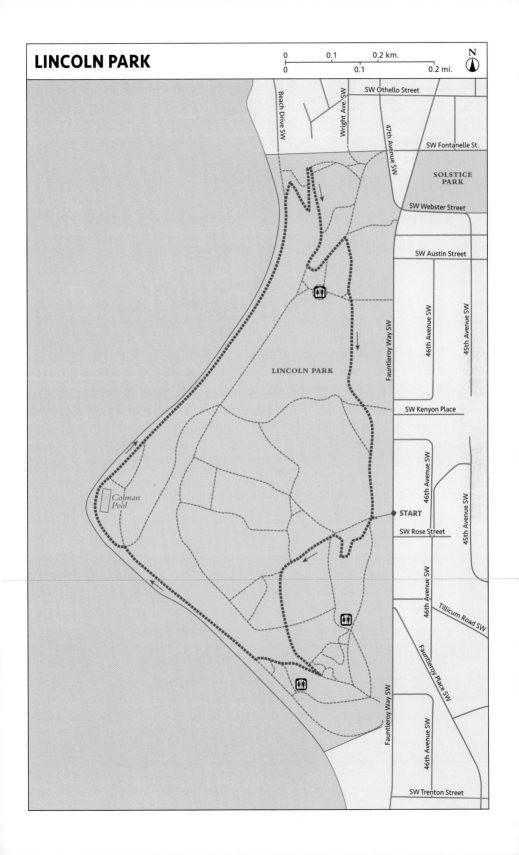

LINCOLN PARK

| 0 | 0.1 | 0.2 km. |
| 0 | 0.1 | 0.2 mi. |

N

Beach Drive SW

Wright Ave. SW

SW Othello Street

47th Avenue SW

SW Fontanelle St.

SOLSTICE
PARK

SW Webster Street

SW Austin Street

46th Avenue SW

45th Avenue SW

Fauntleroy Way SW

LINCOLN PARK

SW Kenyon Place

46th Avenue SW

45th Avenue SW

Colman
Pool

START

SW Rose Street

45th Avenue SW

46th Avenue SW

Tillicum Road SW

Fauntleroy Place SW

Fauntleroy Way SW

46th Avenue SW

SW Trenton Street

STRENGTH TRAINING

THE IMAGE OF A ROAD RUNNER IS OFTEN THAT OF THE ECTOMORPH—somewhat bony with elongated muscles and perhaps a sunken chest. Without besmirching those who restrict their running to paved surfaces, it can be said that trail runners tend to be a bit more muscular and "shapely" than their roadie equivalents. Many reasons account for the differences, but an important one concerns the trail runner's proclivity to vary exercise and recreation routines with other sports, many of which build strength and use the runner's upper body.

When not running, trail runners tend to gravitate toward recreational activities such as backpacking, rock climbing, swimming or pool running, mountain biking, kayaking, backcountry skiing, rollerblading, or even

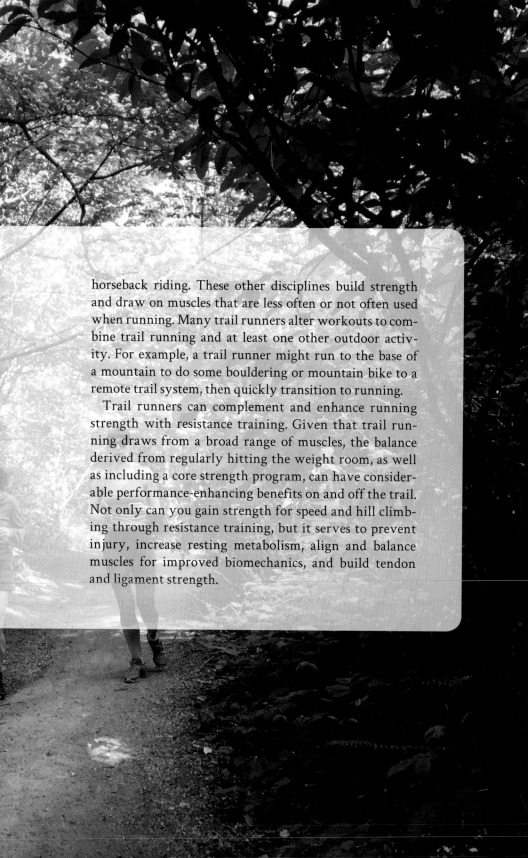

horseback riding. These other disciplines build strength and draw on muscles that are less often or not often used when running. Many trail runners alter workouts to combine trail running and at least one other outdoor activity. For example, a trail runner might run to the base of a mountain to do some bouldering or mountain bike to a remote trail system, then quickly transition to running.

Trail runners can complement and enhance running strength with resistance training. Given that trail running draws from a broad range of muscles, the balance derived from regularly hitting the weight room, as well as including a core strength program, can have considerable performance-enhancing benefits on and off the trail. Not only can you gain strength for speed and hill climbing through resistance training, but it serves to prevent injury, increase resting metabolism, align and balance muscles for improved biomechanics, and build tendon and ligament strength.

Lincoln Park.
PHOTO BY NANCY HOBBS

west down steps to the North Shore Trail. This trail runs along the beach-front of Puget Sound and is partially shaded at the start, then continues as the South Shore Trail, which is mostly paved with no shade. There is a singletrack trail on the grass running adjacent to the South Shore Trail for much of the way. Turn left after the picnic shelters well before the stop for the ferry, which travels to Vashon Island, in the distance. At that juncture, head uphill on a sidewalk and ascend to the top of the pathway, then turn left to follow mostly singletrack trails in and out of the forest back to the parking lot.

NORTH OF SEATTLE

DECEPTION PASS STATE PARK

THIS MASSIVE PARK OFFERS MORE THAN 4,100 ACRES WITH 38 MILES OF trails. The address is 41020 WA 20, Oak Harbor, WA 98277.

GOOSE ROCK PERIMETER TRAIL

THE RUN DOWN

START: At the bottom of the steps on the north side of the first parking lot over the bridge; elevation 122 feet

OVERALL DISTANCE: 3.9-mile lollipop

APPROXIMATE RUNNING TIME: 50 minutes

DIFFICULTY: Blue

ELEVATION GAIN: 960 feet

BEST SEASON TO RUN: Year-round

DOG FRIENDLY: No dogs allowed

PARKING: A day-use fee is charged; an annual Discover Pass is also available, which is good at all Washington state parks

OTHER USERS: Equestrians; mountain bikers on designated trails

CELL PHONE COVERAGE: Good, but may come up as international calling plan (Canada)

MORE INFORMATION: http://parks.state.wa.us/497/Deception-Pass

FINDING THE TRAILHEAD

Head north from Seattle on I-5 and take exit 230 on WA 20 W. Park at the first lot located just after crossing the bridge. Toilets are available in the parking lot, and there is ample parking. The trailhead is located

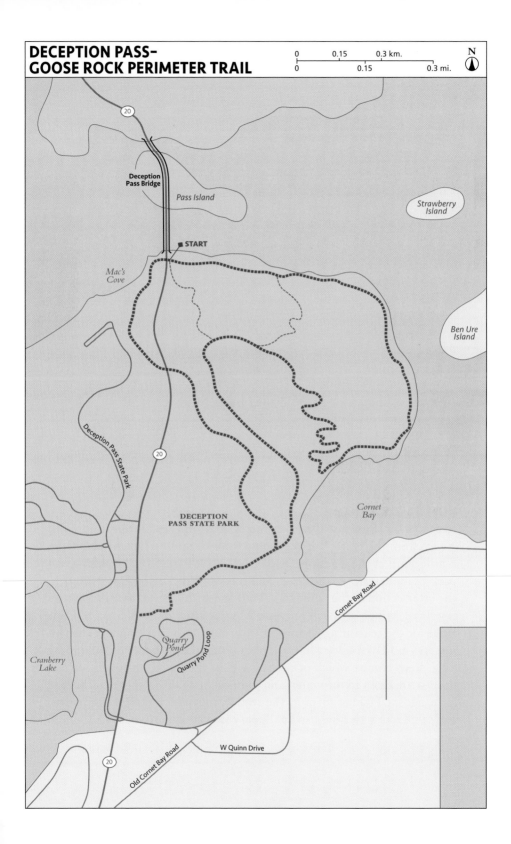

DECEPTION PASS–
GOOSE ROCK PERIMETER TRAIL

0   0.15   0.3 km.
0   0.15   0.3 mi.

N

20

**Deception
Pass Bridge**

Pass Island

*Strawberry
Island*

■ START

*Mac's
Cove*

*Ben Ure
Island*

Deception Pass State Park

20

*Cornet
Bay*

DECEPTION
PASS STATE PARK

Cornet Bay Road

*Quarry
Pond*

Quarry Pond Loop

*Cranberry
Lake*

20

Old Cornet Bay Road

W Quinn Drive

Deception Pass Perimeter Trail.
PHOTO BY NANCY HOBBS

at the bottom of the steps, which are at the north side of the parking lot (closest to the bridge).

RUN DESCRIPTION
Head east on the Goose Rock Perimeter Trail and after 1 mile, turn right (away from the water) on the Goose Rock Summit Trail. At about the 2-mile point at the junction, follow the Lower Forest Trail reaching, the park headquarters on the road. Backtrack on the Lower Forest Trail to the intersection of the Discovery Trail and turn left. Follow the Discovery Trail, which crosses the road (WA 20) after about 3. 5 miles. Continue for the remaining 0.5 mile of this route to the parking lot. The run features mostly singletrack trail, with some technical sections and some long, steep climbs. Much of the route is in the forest, although some is open with views to the water, and some sections at the upper reaches are in meadows. Puddles form in the sections outside of the forested areas, and some rocky sections can be slippery in wet conditions.

DOUBLE LOLLIPOP LOOPS

THE RUN DOWN

START: At the trailhead in the northwest corner of the parking lot off Bowman Bay Road; elevation 10 feet

OVERALL DISTANCE: 3.4 miles on two lollipops

APPROXIMATE RUNNING TIME: 45 minutes

DIFFICULTY: Blue

ELEVATION GAIN: 498 feet

BEST SEASON TO RUN: Year-round

DOG FRIENDLY: No dogs allowed

PARKING: A day-use fee is charged; an annual Discover Pass is also available, which is good at all Washington state parks

OTHER USERS: Equestrians; mountain bikers on some trails in the park

CELL PHONE COVERAGE: Good, but may come up as international calling plan (Canada)

MORE INFORMATION: http://parks.state.wa.us/497/Deception-Pass

Double Lollipop Loops.
PHOTO BY NANCY HOBBS

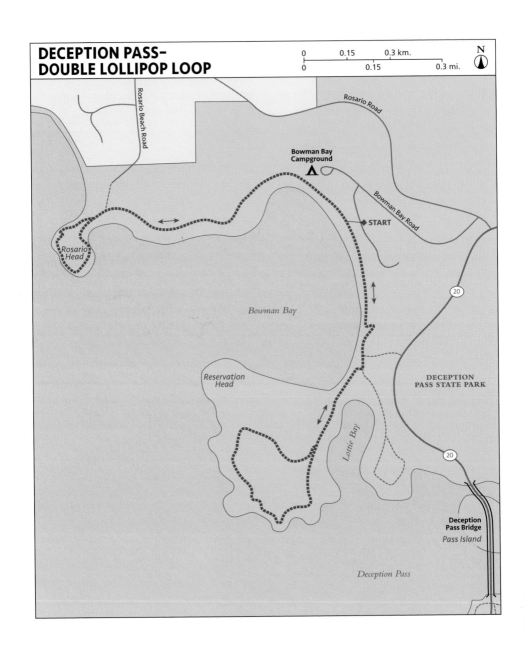

DECEPTION PASS–
DOUBLE LOLLIPOP LOOP

0   0.15   0.3 km.

0   0.15   0.3 mi.

N

Rosario Road

Rosario Beach Road

Bowman Bay
Campground

Bowman Bay Road

START

Rosario
Head

Bowman Bay

20

Reservation
Head

DECEPTION
PASS STATE PARK

Lottie Bay

20

Deception
Pass Bridge

Pass Island

Deception Pass

FINDING THE TRAILHEAD

From WA 20 heading north, turn left on Rosario Road and take an immediate left on Bowman Bay Road. Parking is located off Bowman Bay Road. The trail starts at the northwest (front right) corner of the parking lot, facing the water, and heads north and west on grass to a singletrack trail.

RUN DESCRIPTION

Begin by following the lollipop loop to Rosario Point past a totem pole, then return to the parking lot and continue to the south on a second lollipop loop on Lighthouse Point Trail. Views of the water abound, and the footing is a mixture of dirt, grass, pine needles, rocky sections, and tree roots. There are some puddles on the trails in open areas and some slick spots on the rocky sections, but these easy, enjoyable loops make for solid year-round training with just a few short technical sections and some climbing.

MUD, SNOW, AND ICE

NO SEATTLE TRAIL-RUNNING GUIDE WORTH ITS SALT would neglect to address mud running, given its prominence. The best way to deal with mud on the trail is to enjoy it and to get as dirty as possible early in the run so you won't worry about it thereafter. Soft mud enables a lower-impact run, especially on the descents, where mud provides a great surface for slowing the pace without stressing joints.

To avoid slipping, it may help to shorten your stride, run more upright than normal, and keep your elbows more angled for lateral balance. If you begin to slip, try to relax and control the recovery so as not to overreact and fall in the opposite direction.

If water is running down the trail, the best bet is to run where water is moving most rapidly because that surface will probably be the most firm. A faster current tends to remove most of the sticky sediment, leaving behind gravel and rock. Although the runner will get wet, the likelihood of getting bogged down in muddier trail borders is markedly decreased. This technique is also friendlier to the trail because of the lower environmental impact.

From an environmental standpoint, resist the temptation to run alongside the trail in an effort to avoid getting muddy. Submitting to the temptation leads to wider trails; and if everyone did it, pathways would soon be major thruways instead of singletrack trails. Typical Puget Sound weather causes muddy trails, and depending on the sensitivity of the specific trail system, it may be advisable to avoid certain trails until they have a chance to dry.

Although they are uncommon in Seattle, snow and ice do occasionally hit the trails. Running with confidence is more important on snow and ice than on any other surface. Although most runners are hesitant on snow and ice, the trick is to try to tuck away that insecurity, take a deep breath, relax, and run with a sense of command. Admittedly, snow and ice, being inanimate elements, cannot read minds; however, they manage to wreak havoc on runners who fear them. Fearful runners run with tense form, lean back, and often resort to jerky, sudden movements in an attempt to adapt to the slick surface. That is just the opposite of what works best for running on slick snow or ice.

The best form for snow and ice running is a slight forward lean that distributes the body's weight evenly across the foot as it hits the slippery surface. Fluid, steady movement is less likely to cause a loss of traction. In the event of slipping on snow or ice, the best response is to relax and to try to let your body flow with a calculated response. Do not try to stop or brake, as that will just cause you to slide out and fall. Resist the impulse to tense up or make a sudden movement to counter the slipping, which all too often leads to slipping even more. Instead, relax and breathe steadily. Even if slipping on snow and ice does lead to a fall, being relaxed will reduce the likelihood of injury. Besides, one of the best benefits of snow is that it cushions the impact.

Snowshoeing and running with crampons or ice spikes are alternatives that make trails accessible no matter how much it snows or whether they are covered by ice. The snow's forgiving compressibility and the impact absorption from snowshoes' increased surface area make it feel as though you are running on wood-chip-lined trails.

SOUTH OF SEATTLE

FORT STEILACOOM PARK

THIS 340-ACRE PARK, LOCATED IN THE CITY OF LAKEWOOD within 40 minutes of Seattle, offers about 7 miles of trails, gravel roadways, and dirt footpaths. In addition to running opportunities, there are picnic areas, sports fields, a playground, and a lake. At first glance, there looks to be just flat terrain, but once you enter the forest, you will find some steep climbs—some with upward of a 20 percent grade—and descents affording some technical terrain and varied training opportunities. In addition to the singletrack, there are some trails through open meadows, as well as a nice, hard-packed gravel route around Waughop Lake.

The trails are not well signed, and it is easy to get turned around; but, despite this, you will soon find your way again because the trails always lead to a familiar pathway or vantage point, where you can reorient yourself to get back on track. There are plenty of entry-level trails with minimal elevation gain. Pair these with steep climbs and descents within the upper reaches of the forest beyond the meadows and sports fields, and the area appeals to runners of all levels.

This park hosts cross-country races in the fall, trail races from 5K to 50K, and has a 5K route mapped on its website. In fact, this venue was suggested by nine-time US Mountain Running Team member Joseph Gray, who grew up in Lakewood. Gray trained extensively in Fort Steilacoom Park.

There are several parking lots in the park, as well as access points from adjacent neighborhoods. Following the run, consider a visit to Primo Coffee Stand, located just minutes from the park on Steilacoom Avenue, or a forage at the nearby Trader Joe's.

SOUTH OF SEATTLE

WATCH YOUR STEP

Some of the trails in this guide are groomed and wide enough that they are practically dirt roads, while others are of the singletrack variety. Some allow dogs, others do not. Some turn into shoe-sucking mud when wet; others become rocky riverbeds. Still others attract local fauna during mating or nesting season. We request that you honor not only notes about trail sensitivities that we've provided in the guide, but also that you be very aware of the conditions and follow Leave No Trace practices in your trail running.

FINGER LOOP 4-MILE

THE RUN DOWN

START: At the trailhead on Dresden Ln. SW; elevation 246 feet

OVERALL DISTANCE: 3.8-mile loop

APPROXIMATE RUNNING TIME: 42 minutes

DIFFICULTY: Blue

ELEVATION GAIN: 321 feet

BEST SEASON TO RUN: Year-round

DOG FRIENDLY: Leashed dogs permitted

PARKING: Free

OTHER USERS: Mountain bikers

CELL PHONE COVERAGE: Good

MORE INFORMATION: www .cityoflakewood.us/parks-and-recreation/parks/fort-steilacoom-park

FINDING THE TRAILHEAD

From Tacoma, head south on I-5 to S 74th Street/Custer Road W. Turn right on 88th Street SW/Steilacoom Boulevard SW. Turn left on 87th Avenue SW to Dresden Lane SW. Park at the lot on Dresden Lane SW. There are many different routes available from this parking lot. For this route, head east across the grassy meadow for the start.

RUN DESCRIPTION

This route enables you to fully experience the park's trails by including flat sections in open grassy meadows; singletrack trails with switchbacks in the forest; roots and rocks; and a mixture of gravel roads. For good measure, there are some steep and short uphills as well as long, sloping downhills, all making this an enjoyable effort. Although this route doesn't continue around the entire lake, you can easily add that to the running distance.

From the start in the grassy meadow, head east, running next to the road, before turning south onto the trails in the meadow. Continue through the forest on single- and doubletrack trails to the far reaches of

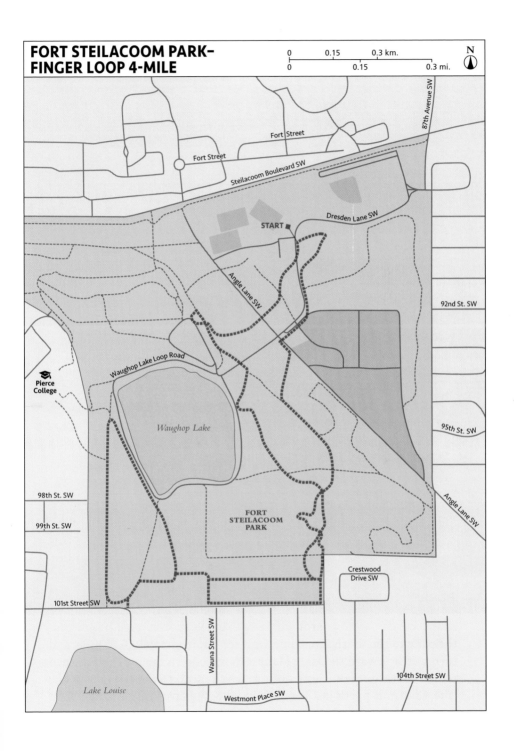

FORT STEILACOOM PARK–
FINGER LOOP 4-MILE

0   0.15   0.3 km.

0   0.15   0.3 mi.

N

Fort Street

Fort Street

Steilacoom Boulevard SW

87th Avenue SW

Dresden Lane SW

START

Angle Lane SW

92nd St. SW

Waughop Lake Loop Road

Pierce College

Waughop Lake

95th St. SW

Angle Lane SW

98th St. SW

99th St. SW

FORT
STEILACOOM
PARK

Crestwood
Drive SW

101st Street SW

Wauna Street SW

104th Street SW

Lake Louise

Westmont Place SW

Finger Loop 4-Mile.
PHOTO BY NANCY HOBBS

the park to the south. Continue west for approximately 0.75 mile, and turn north toward the lake. Make a short loop to the northwest, then return south to the turnoff and retrace the trail to the east side of the lake. Continue north just beyond the lake, and cross Angie Lane SW to the Dresden Lane parking lot.

FORT STEILACOOM PARK 5K LOOP

THE RUN DOWN

START: The parking lot on Dresden Ln. SW; elevation 246 feet

OVERALL DISTANCE: 3.1-mile loop

APPROXIMATE RUNNING TIME: 30 minutes

DIFFICULTY: Green

ELEVATION GAIN: 321 feet

BEST SEASON TO RUN: Year-round

DOG FRIENDLY: Leashed dogs permitted

PARKING: Free

OTHER USERS: Mountain bikers

CELL PHONE COVERAGE: Good

MORE INFORMATION: www .cityoflakewood.us/parks-and-recreation/parks/fort-steilacoom-park

FINDING THE TRAILHEAD

 Park at the lot on Dresden Lane SW.

Fort Steilacoom Park 5K Loop.
PHOTO BY NANCY HOBBS

FORT STEILACOOM PARK-5K

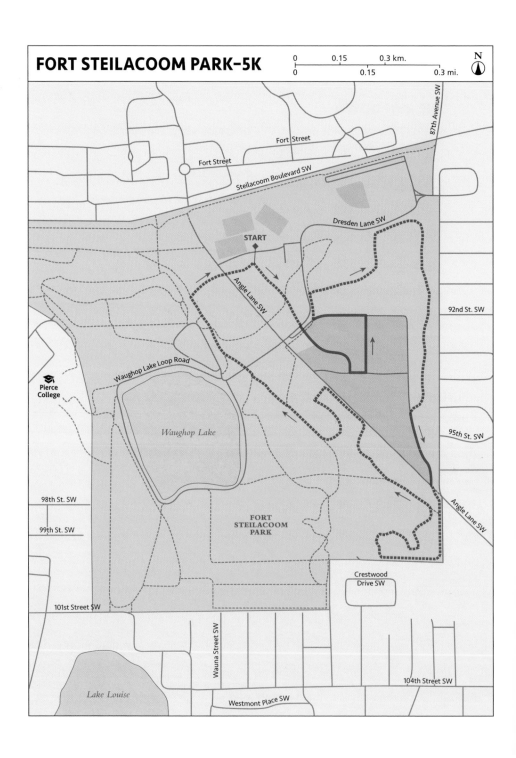

Fort Street

Fort Street

Steilacoom Boulevard SW

Dresden Lane SW

87th Avenue SW

START

Angle Lane SW

92nd St. SW

Waughop Lake Loop Road

Pierce College

Waughop Lake

95th St. SW

Angle Lane SW

98th St. SW

99th St. SW

FORT STEILACOOM PARK

Crestwood Drive SW

101st Street SW

Wauna Street SW

104th Street SW

Lake Louise

Westmont Place SW

N

0   0.15   0.3 km.

0   0.15   0.3 mi.

RUN DESCRIPTION

Start in the grassy meadow by the pavilion, and head east toward the barns. Cross the road onto a crushed gravel path, winding around the dog park on flat trails. Follow the trail adjacent to the paved road and enter the woods, running on enjoyable singletrack terrain with some climbing and descending on short, tight switchbacks. Watch for roots peeking out from the downed leaves.

Continue through the forest on rolling terrain, and turn right out of the woods at a noticeable clearing. Follow this trail to the road (on the west side of the park), and finish just beyond the parking lot in the grassy field where the loop began.

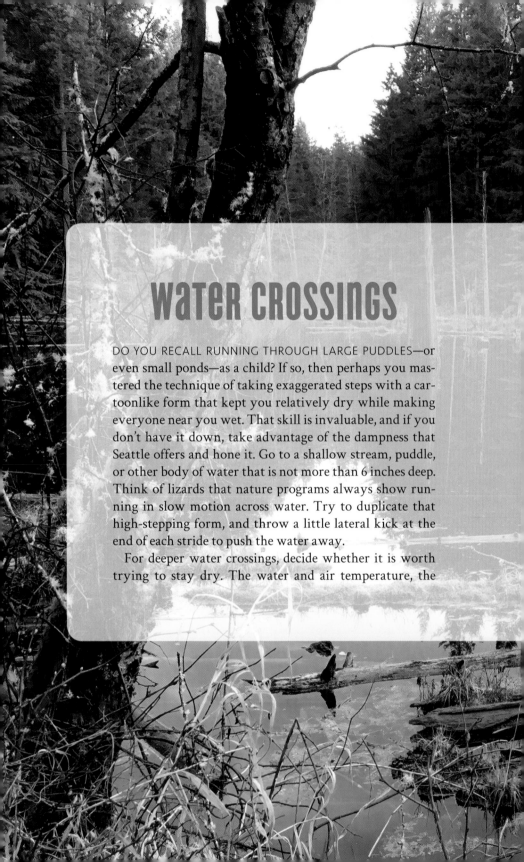

WaTeR CROSSINGS

DO YOU RECALL RUNNING THROUGH LARGE PUDDLES—or even small ponds—as a child? If so, then perhaps you mastered the technique of taking exaggerated steps with a cartoonlike form that kept you relatively dry while making everyone near you wet. That skill is invaluable, and if you don't have it down, take advantage of the dampness that Seattle offers and hone it. Go to a shallow stream, puddle, or other body of water that is not more than 6 inches deep. Think of lizards that nature programs always show running in slow motion across water. Try to duplicate that high-stepping form, and throw a little lateral kick at the end of each stride to push the water away.

For deeper water crossings, decide whether it is worth trying to stay dry. The water and air temperature, the

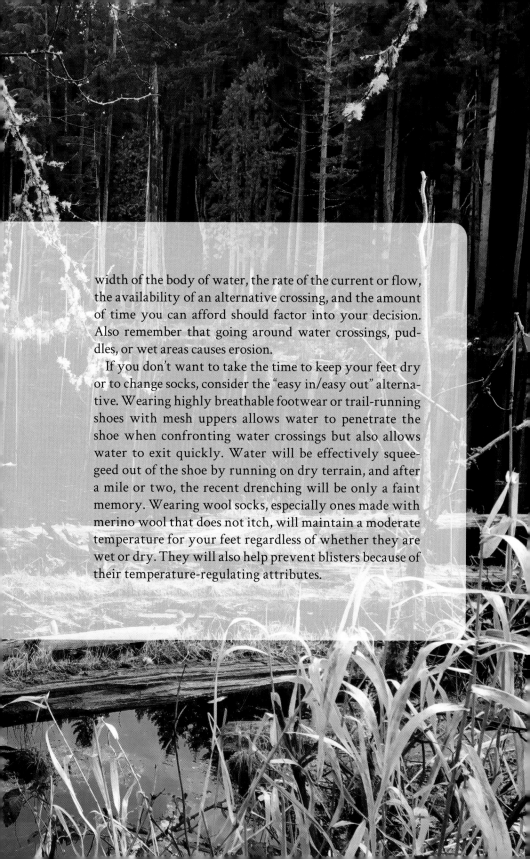

width of the body of water, the rate of the current or flow, the availability of an alternative crossing, and the amount of time you can afford should factor into your decision. Also remember that going around water crossings, puddles, or wet areas causes erosion.

If you don't want to take the time to keep your feet dry or to change socks, consider the "easy in/easy out" alternative. Wearing highly breathable footwear or trail-running shoes with mesh uppers allows water to penetrate the shoe when confronting water crossings but also allows water to exit quickly. Water will be effectively squeegeed out of the shoe by running on dry terrain, and after a mile or two, the recent drenching will be only a faint memory. Wearing wool socks, especially ones made with merino wool that does not itch, will maintain a moderate temperature for your feet regardless of whether they are wet or dry. They will also help prevent blisters because of their temperature-regulating attributes.

POINT DEFIANCE PARK

IN THE METRO PARKS TACOMA SYSTEM, this multi-activity space encompasses 702 acres and includes a zoo, an aquarium, botanical gardens, a promenade along the beach, and the Fort Nisqually Living History Museum. The nearly 10 miles of trails include well-signed primary routes and not-as-well-signed secondary singletrack trails. The Five Mile Drive outer loop roadway is closed to vehicular traffic on weekends until 1 p.m., and Monday through Friday until 10 a.m. Bicycling on the paved road is permissible.

4.5-MILE LOOP

THE RUN DOWN

START: On the Spine Trail; elevation 29 feet

OVERALL DISTANCE: 4.5-mile loop

APPROXIMATE RUNNING TIME: 50 minutes

DIFFICULTY: Green

ELEVATION GAIN: 483 feet

BEST SEASON TO RUN: Year-round

DOG FRIENDLY: Leashed dogs permitted

PARKING: Free

OTHER USERS: None

CELL PHONE COVERAGE: Good

MORE INFORMATION: www.metroparkstacoma.org/point-defiance-park/

FINDING THE TRAILHEAD

From Seattle, follow I-5 south to Bantz Boulevard exit 132B to WA 16 W. Turn right on N Pearl Street. Turn left on N 51st Street and continue straight on Mildred Street. Enter the park on the one-way Five Mile Drive and follow the road to signs for Owen Beach. Park in the lot near Owen Beach, where you'll find restrooms, and start the run by

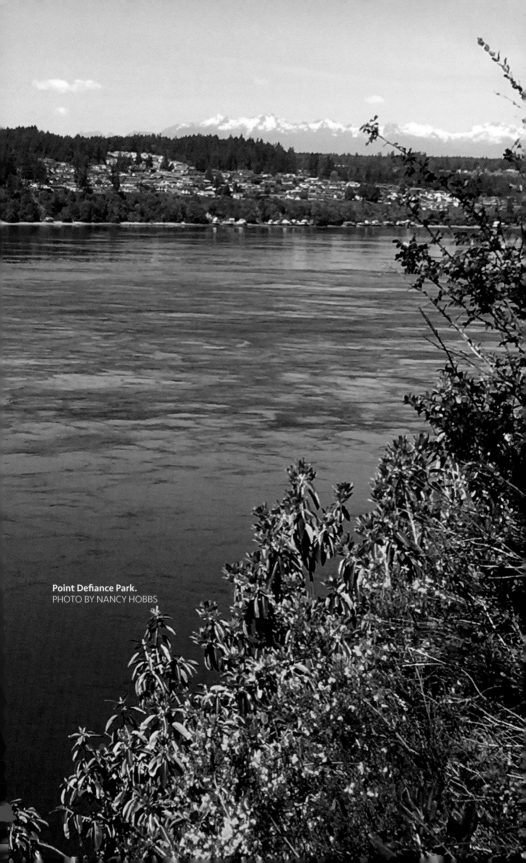

Point Defiance Park.
PHOTO BY NANCY HOBBS

POINT DEFIANCE PARK

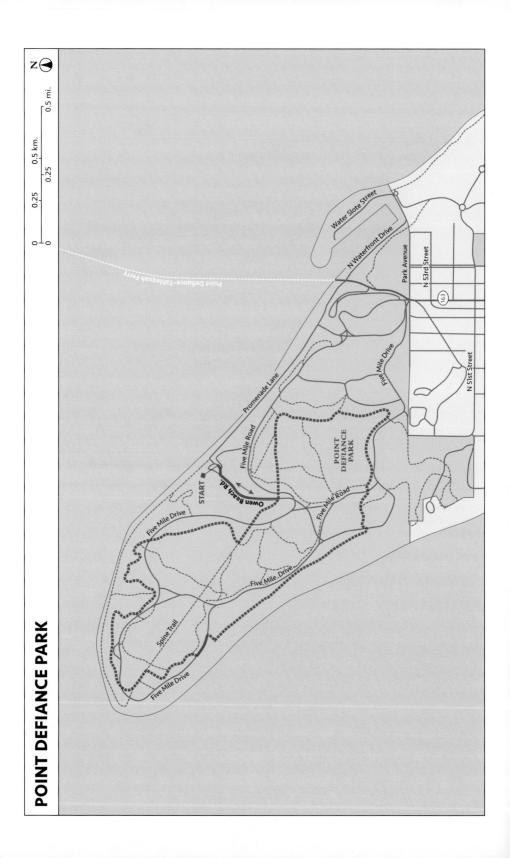

Point Defiance Park.
PHOTO BY NANCY HOBBS

proceeding up the paved road (N Owen Beach Road), heading away from the water. Enter the forest on a singletrack trail about 0.25 mile up the road on the left.

RUN DESCRIPTION

The signage at the run's entry point indicates the Spine Trail. Follow this singletrack route, which connects to the Outer Loop Trail. Along the Outside Loop, there is a bit of climbing and descending. Although serene and peaceful, the trail is never far from the Five Mile Drive, which you will cross several times during the run, first at the 1.25-mile point. The views along the west side of the route include Gig Harbor, and on the east side, Vashon Island and Puget Sound. Although some of the secondary trails are not as well maintained, there is nothing too technical, and any rocky and rooted sections are short.

DASH POINT STATE PARK

WITH 11 MILES OF METICULOUSLY MARKED TRAILS, this park begs for exploration. Not only are there a variety of trails weaving in and out of the woods, over footbridges, up steps, and around switchbacks, but there is also a beach on the north side of the park with unobstructed views of Puget Sound. There are campsites for an extended visit or picnic areas where you can enjoy a postrun meal, provided you packed your provisions.

6-MILE TOUR

THE RUN DOWN

START: Raven Beach Trail; elevation 214 feet

OVERALL DISTANCE: 5.7-mile double loop

APPROXIMATE RUNNING TIME: 70 minutes

DIFFICULTY: Blue

ELEVATION GAIN: 600 feet

BEST SEASON TO RUN: Year-round

DOG FRIENDLY: Leashed dogs permitted

PARKING: A day-use fee is charged; an annual Discover Pass is also available, which is good at all Washington state parks

OTHER USERS: Bikers on designated trails; no equestrians

CELL PHONE: Poor in some sections, good in others

MORE INFORMATION: http://parks.state.wa.us/496/Dash-Point

FINDING THE TRAILHEAD

From Seattle, go south on I-5 to S 320th Street in Federal Way. Continue to SW Dash Point Road. The park's address is 5700 SW Dash Point Road in Federal Way, just east of Spring Street NE and west of 55th Avenue SW. Once inside the toll booth, turn right and park at the ranger

Dash Point State Park 5.7 Mile.
PHOTO BY NANCY HOBBS

station. To reach the trailhead, turn right from the ranger station on the road, keep to the left shoulder, and follow the road about 0.25 mile to the Raven Beach Trail. You can also start in the parking lot at the Raven Beach Trail, but if you have valuables in view in the vehicle, it is best to park at the ranger station to avoid vandalism.

RUN DESCRIPTION

After a short run down to the parking lot on the Raven Beach Trail, cross the parking lot and head west to the trailhead for the Thames Creek (Beach) Trail. This trail is wide and starts out on hard-packed gravel. Cross several footbridges and ascend steps across Thames Creek, enjoying the peaceful surroundings and excellent photo opportunities at this well-crafted bridge.

DASH POINT STATE PARK–5.7 MILE

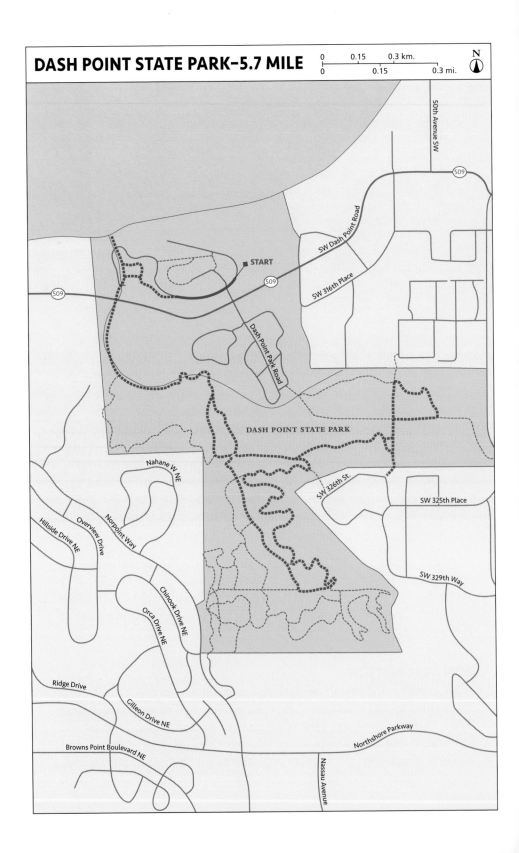

Continue over the bridge and up the steps on the other side of the creek to the Outbound Trail. From here the majority of trails are singletrack, with some exposed roots and numerous leaves carpeting the trail. Some puddles may pool after a decent rain, but muddy spots don't tend to linger.

Connect to the Boundary Trail, which meets Shannon's Shin Trail, and head north to enjoy the aptly named Switchback Trail for a quick 0.5-mile loop. Note: There is a short section on Hoyt Road Trail that dead-ends at Hoyt Road in a neighborhood to the east. This is an access point for the park that does not require a parking fee or pass.

Return on Shannon's Shin and retrace the Boundary Trail to meet with the Log Jam Trail heading south. Complete with switchbacks and climbing, this is a great section of trail that connects to another singletrack, the IMBA Trail. Follow the IMBA Trail to the Ridge Trail and head east, making a longer loop that can include several finger trails (Night Crawler, Toenail, TNT, the "S," Technical Trail, and Kate's Creek). Or, as this marked route suggests, head west and continue to the Double Dip Trail, joining with Heart Attack Hill to head north. In this direction the Heart Attack section is downhill.

At the intersection with the East Rim and Outbound Trails, pick either route back to the Thames Creek (Beach) Trail. Finish the run with a quick out-and-back run to the beach before heading back to the Raven Beach Trail, which will be uphill back to the car.

After the run, drive a short way to BigFoot Java, located on SW 320th Street, for some energy replacement.

3-MILE LOOP FROM NORPOINT WAY NE

THE RUN DOWN

START: Off Norpoint Way NE near the Tacoma Water District property; elevation 430 feet

OVERALL DISTANCE: 3 miles

APPROXIMATE RUNNING TIME: 30 minutes

DIFFICULTY: Blue

ELEVATION GAIN: 233 feet

BEST SEASON TO RUN: Year-round

DOG FRIENDLY: Leashed dogs permitted

PARKING: Free on-street parking

OTHER USERS: No equestrians; cyclists on designated trails

CELL PHONE COVERAGE: Good

MORE INFORMATION: http://parks.state.wa.us/496/Dash-Point

FINDING THE TRAILHEAD

In Federal Way, go west on SW Dash Point Road to East Side Drive NE, turn left onto 21st Avenue NE, and then turn left on Norpoint Way NE. Park near the Tacoma Water District property. The trail starts just east of Norpoint Way NE.

RUN DESCRIPTION

This route encompasses some of the same trails as the longer route, but stays on the southern side of the park. Singletrack trails with rolling terrain make this an enjoyable, albeit short, run.

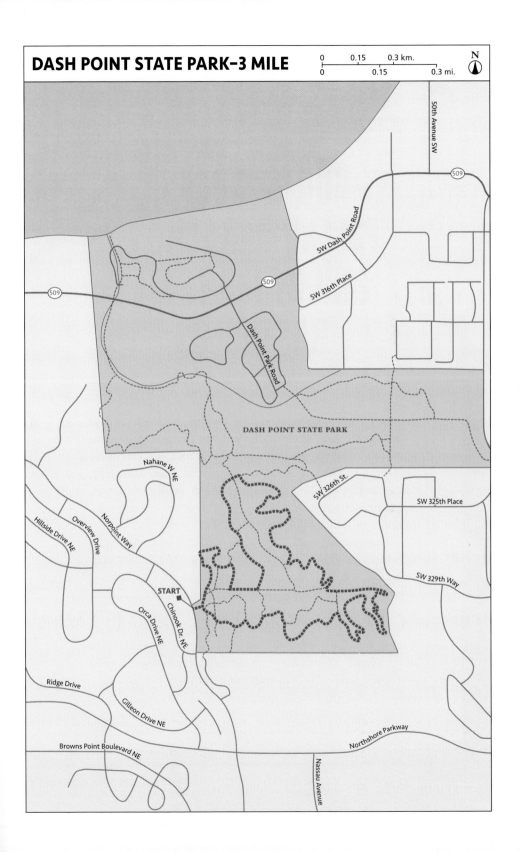

DASH POINT STATE PARK–3 MILE

| 0 | 0.15 | 0.3 km. |
| 0 | 0.15 | 0.3 mi. |

N

50th Avenue SW

509

SW Dash Point Road

SW 316th Place

509

509

Dash Point Park Road

DASH POINT STATE PARK

SW 326th St.

SW 325th Place

Nahane W NE

SW 329th Way

Overview Drive

Norpoint Way

Hillside Drive NE

START

Chinook Dr. NE

Orca Drive NE

Ridge Drive

Gilleon Drive NE

Browns Point Boulevard NE

Northshore Parkway

Nassau Avenue

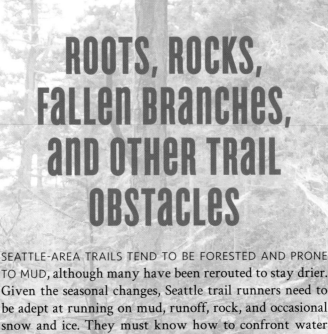

ROOTS, ROCKS, FALLEN BRANCHES, AND OTHER TRAIL OBSTACLES

SEATTLE-AREA TRAILS TEND TO BE FORESTED AND PRONE TO MUD, although many have been rerouted to stay drier. Given the seasonal changes, Seattle trail runners need to be adept at running on mud, runoff, rock, and occasional snow and ice. They must know how to confront water crossings and when to avoid dangerous ones. Similarly, they must be capable of maneuvering around roots, rocks, fallen branches, and dealing with other trail obstacles and handling wildlife confrontations.

When running on a particularly difficult section of trail, it is often beneficial to lift your knees a little higher than usual. This will give your feet more ground clearance to avoid catching a toe or otherwise tripping on a rock, root, or other potential snag. Using the forward vision technique, where your eyes are steps ahead of your feet, anticipating or "setting up" for upcoming obstacles on trail descents, helps select a line in the trail that, in turn, helps to maintain speed without losing balance or twisting an ankle.

Depending on running style, the length of the run, and the distance traveled, trail runners may find it easiest to use a shorter stride and to run through rough footing with lighter but more rapid steps. Running on your forefoot, the way football players—hardly known for their daintiness—run through tire obstacle courses, takes weight off your feet so you can quickly adjust your balance and recover from any misstep. Of course, this is difficult to do when tired and legs and feet feel heavy and sluggish.

Trail runners will probably always wonder whether it is best to jump over, go around, or step on top of a fallen tree, branch, rock, or other obstacle blocking the most direct line of travel along a trail. Even though the decision to jump is driven by numerous factors, trail runners must make the choice instantaneously. Some of the more substantial variables in the equation are the speed at which you approach the obstacle, the size and stability of the obstacle, your general agility and experience, the footing leading to and from the obstacle, and your general level of chutzpah or cunning.

Once you've made the lightning-fast decision of whether to go over or around an obstacle, embrace it with confidence, then leap over, step on, or steer around the barrier without second-guessing the decision. Don't dwell on a botched decision, but learn from mistakes so you are better able to tackle the next trail barrier. The element of surprise, the challenge of uncertainty, and the never-ending supply of different obstacles are what make trail running exciting. If these uncertainties do not make for fun and excitement, run roads.

EAST OF SEATTLE

MERCER SLOUGH NATURE PARK

THIS 320-ACRE PARK OFFERS 7 MILES OF WELL-SIGNED TRAILS in an urban setting within the city limits of Bellevue and provides a variety of terrain, from wide, crushed gravel paths along open meadows to singletrack trails, and includes boardwalks, steps, climbing, and descending in the forest. In addition, a sidewalk trail runs the periphery of the park. There are several access points from the east, where the Mercer Slough Environmental Education Center is located, and from the west, where the Winters House Visitor Center and a seasonal blueberry farm are located.

MERCER SLOUGH NATURE PARK

THE RUN DOWN

START: Elevation 30 feet

OVERALL DISTANCE: 5 miles of multiple loops

APPROXIMATE RUNNING TIME: 50 minutes

DIFFICULTY: Green

ELEVATION GAIN: 183 feet

BEST SEASON TO RUN: Year-round

DOG FRIENDLY: Dogs on a leash

PARKING: Free

OTHER USERS: Cyclists

CELL PHONE COVERAGE: Very good

MORE INFORMATION: www.ci.bellevue.wa.us/mercer_slough.htm

FINDING THE TRAILHEAD

From Seattle, follow I-90 E to Bellevue Way SE (exit 9). Continue on Bellevue Way SE and Park at the Winters House Visitor Center, 2102 Bellevue Way SE.

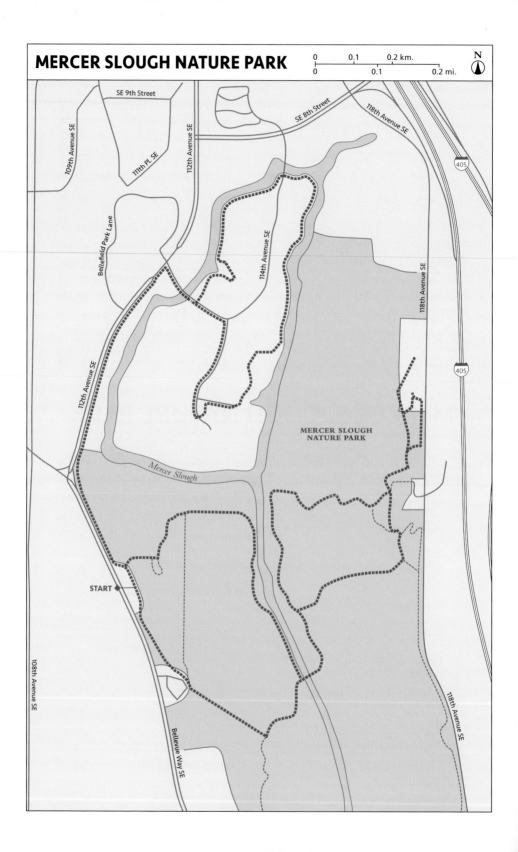

MERCER SLOUGH NATURE PARK

0   0.1   0.2 km.
0   0.1   0.2 mi.

N

SE 9th Street

109th Avenue SE

111th Pl. SE

112th Avenue SE

SE 8th Street

118th Avenue SE

405

Bellefield Park Lane

114th Avenue SE

118th Avenue SE

405

112th Avenue SE

Mercer Slough

MERCER SLOUGH
NATURE PARK

START

108th Avenue SE

Bellevue Way SE

118th Avenue SE

Mercer Slough Nature Park.
PHOTO BY NANCY HOBBS

RUN DESCRIPTION

Start on the Heritage Trail, just steps from the interpretive kiosk and the Winters House Visitor Center. Follow this crushed gravel path, which travels alongside an open meadow before reaching a boardwalk and footbridge across Mercer Slough. Continue to the Bellefields Loop Trail, and turn right on this mostly singletrack path, which features intermittent exposed roots, a few steps, and rolling terrain. Reach the Mercer Slough Environmental Education Center after about 1 mile, following a portion of the Lake-to-Lake Trail (a 10-mile multiuse trail connecting nine parks across Bellevue).

Return on the Bellefields Loop Trail, crossing back over the Mercer Slough, and turn left on the Heritage Trail to return to the start point after 2.5 miles. This mapped route continues past the parking lot on the Heritage Trail, turning left to enjoy some urban running along Bellevue Way SE. Turn right on 112th Avenue SE for a loop around an office park on SE 15th Street, by the Mercer Slough on a mostly doubletrack path, then return to the start point. For a longer journey, continue north on 112th Avenue SE, turning right on SE 8th Street, and right on 118th Avenue SE to lead back to the education center. Continue for another few miles through the park back to the start point.

STRETCHING

ALTHOUGH ATHLETES HAVE FOCUSED ON FLEXIBILITY FOR DECADES, coaches and trainers have only recently begun stressing the importance of stretching, although some discourage the practice.

Stretching used to be something smiling people wearing leotards did in black-and-white television programs while they bounced in what has become an antiquated school of ballistic stretching: "And one...two...three...." Since those days, the art of stretching has grown dramatically, and trail runners may now choose between myriad techniques.

Stretching is fundamental to gaining and sustaining flexibility, which is a crucial element of trail running. By maintaining a regular stretching routine, trail runners are able to avoid injury by helping their muscles, tendons, and ligaments remain supple. Stretching staves off the stiffness and rigidity brought on by training and racing and increases elasticity and resilience of connective tissues. Stretching also aids in recovery, injury prevention, stride length, strength, and nimbleness on the trail.

There is great diversity in stretching philosophies, and each school of thought has its own set of guidelines. The following recommendations for the trail runner were gleaned from an examination of these various approaches to stretching:

- Warm up before stretching. Warm muscles are less prone to strains, pulls, rips, or other injuries. Depending on the outside temperature, the location of the warm-up, the particular warm-up exercise, and its intensity, the prestretch period should equal approximately the time you would take to cover a flat mile. Do some stretching after the run to prevent post-workout soreness.

- Use proper form to isolate particular target muscles. If questions arise about how to go about a specific stretching routine, take a stretching class at a local health club or recreation center, consult with a personal trainer or coach, or check a book on stretching. Bob Anderson's 1975 book, *Stretching*, remains one of the better texts on the subject. Build a repertoire of stretches that addresses your particular needs, and stick to it as a regular part of your training schedule.

- Don't bounce. Ballistic stretching triggers a reflex that has the effect of tightening muscles. Ballistic stretching may also lead to a strain or other damage caused by bouncing beyond the natural range of motion. Using a long, sustained, static stretch after warming up releases tension that has built up in the area of focus.

- Isolate particular muscles that are the goal of a particular stretch, and "breathe" into specific muscles as you feel slow elongations of the targeted area. Stay relaxed and use slow rhythmic breathing. Hands, feet, shoulders, jaw, and face should not reflect tension.

- Continue the stretch to the point where a slight pull is felt, but not to the point of pain. According to Anderson, a mild comfortable stretch should result in tension that can be felt without pain. Do not gauge a stretch by how far you can reach; go by feel alone.

- If susceptible to particular types of injury or if you are currently injured, pay special attention to stretching that area. In some cases, stretching may make the injury worse or prolong recovery. It may be worth consulting an expert before engaging in any stretching routine while injured.

- When performing a static pose, hold the stretch for as long as 30 seconds and stretch both sides equally. Anderson recommends that when doing a stretch, you should feel comfortable enough with the tension that it can be held for 10 to 25 seconds, after which the initial feeling of the stretch should subside or disappear. That kind of stretching reduces muscle tension and maintains flexibility.

- To increase flexibility, Anderson recommends a "developmental stretch." After an easy stretch to the point where the feeling of tension dissipates, go into the pose again—but go deeper—until increased tension is felt. The stretch should not feel any more intense when held 10 to 30 seconds. If it does, ease off to a more comfortable position.

Incorporate the above rules as you customize a stretching routine that fits and appeals to your particular needs.

Consider incorporating some of the following stretches into your stretching regimen as a trail runner. These suggestions are by no means exhaustive, and it is recommended that additional resources be consulted to select and perfect an appropriate personal stretching routine.

Hamstrings: A modified hurdler's stretch involves sitting with one leg bent and that foot tucked against the inside of the thigh of the extended leg. From that position, lean forward (keeping the back straight) from the hips to touch with one or both hands the foot of the extended leg, reaching until tension is felt in the hamstring of the extended leg. Another hamstring stretch is to lie flat on your back, lift one leg and pull it toward the chest, with the other leg bent and its foot planted straight in front. A third hamstring stretch is to stand with one leg raised so that the foot rests on a solid object, such as a stool or a rock that is about at knee level. With the standing leg slightly bent, lean forward from the hips, keeping the back straight, and reach for the ankle of the extended leg until stretch is felt in the hamstring of the extended leg.

Iliotibial (IT) Band: The IT band stretches from just behind the hip, down the side of the leg, and connects to the top of the shin. When the IT band tightens, it can cause a flare-up on the side of the knee, resulting in pain. If a runner persists in running with a problematic IT band, it can ultimately seize up like an engine that has run dry of lubrication.

Any one—or all—of the following stretches can keep the IT band loose and flexible. In a sitting position with both legs stretched in front, cross one leg over the other and cradle the crossed leg in your arms, pulling the shin and foot of the crossed leg toward the chest until a stretch is felt in the hip of the bent leg. For a deeper stretch, cross the other leg over the extended leg, placing the foot of the bent leg on the other side of the extended leg, and place the opposite elbow against the bent knee (for example, if the left leg is bent, place the right elbow against the left side of the left knee), and press against the bent knee until the stretch is felt. Or, from a standing position, cross one leg in front of the other and lean forward to touch the toes until tension is felt in the hip of the rear leg. In the same pose, stand more upright and lean into the hip of the rear leg until tension is felt.

Groin: Because trail runners consistently have to dodge obstacles on the trail, they must incorporate considerably more lateral motion than do road runners. Sudden movement from side to side can lead to a pull or strain in the groin, unless that area is properly limber. One easy stretch is to sit down, pull both heels into the groin, and place the soles of both feet against each other, with knees close to or touching the ground. Increase the tension of the stretch by pulling the heels closer to the body or lowering the knees to the ground by pressing elbows against knees.

Quadriceps: Descending a rocky trail at a fast pace places considerable stress on the quadriceps. A number of stretches can be performed to loosen your quads. One easy stretch is to stand on one foot and bend the other leg backward, reaching back with both hands to hold the foot of the bent leg, lifting the foot to the point where a stretch is felt. Another stretch is one that should not be performed by those with weak ankles or problem knees; if in doubt, consult an expert. Kneel on the ground with both knees, feet pointed backward and tucked underneath. Lean backward until the quads feel a stretch. Another basic quad exercise that helps build flexibility is to perform a static squat by slowly bending the knees while keeping the back straight and your weight centered over your pelvis.

Calves: Nonrunners often chuckle at the sight of runners who appear to be trying to push over a building or lamppost. Little do the nonrunners know that the runner is merely stretching calf muscles. This stretch involves standing about arm's length from a wall, post, tree, rock, or other fixed object and placing both hands against the object. Bend one leg off the ground as the other leg is stretched straight behind, keeping the heel of the straightened leg on the ground with the toes facing forward. Lean into the rear leg until that calf is stretched.

Devoting substantial time stretching calves may be well worth the investment, especially if focus is on the full range of the gastrocnemius muscles. Maintaining calf flexibility is very important for trail runners, who tend to run high on their toes or do a lot of hill work. For those limber enough to touch their toes, another way to stretch the calves is to sit on the ground and extend both legs parallel straight in front. Lean forward from the hips with the back straight and hold the toes, pulling them toward the body until a stretch is felt in the calves. If you cannot touch your toes, loop a band or towel around your toes, then pull on it to stretch the calves.

Ankles and Achilles Tendons: One of the greatest problem areas for trail runners is weak ankles. Maintaining flexible ankles helps prevent ankle rolls or sprains and enables you to recover from what could be a calamity. Ankle rotations are easy to perform and can be done even while sitting. Lift one foot a few inches off the ground and slowly rotate it through its full range of motion. Rotate in both directions. To stretch the Achilles tendon, stand with one leg raised so that its heel rests on a solid object that is about at knee level. Lean forward, place both hands under the ball of your raised foot, and gradually pull toward the body. After feeling the stretch, point the toes toward the ground as far as possible.

Back and Trunk: Trail runners should invest heavily in a limber back and trunk. A tight back or midsection can lead to a nightmare of injuries, terrible running form, and an unhealthy posture. Practicing yoga on a regular basis can lead to a flexible back and relaxed running form. Back and trunk stretches include a standing waist twist, where hips are rotated in one direction as you look over your shoulder and hold the stretch, with hands on hips, knees slightly bent, and feet pointed forward. For a standing back extension stretch from the same standing position, place palms just above the hips with fingers pointing down, then slowly push the palms forward to create an extension in the lower back, and hold the stretch.

Another easy back stretch, which releases tension that may build up from running hills or rocky trails, is to lie on your back and bend your knees, lifting them slowly toward your chest until you can clasp your hands around the shins. Keep pulling the knees into the chest until the lower back feels stretched. An additional lower back stretch involves lying on your back with one leg extended flat on the ground. Bend the knee of the other leg and cross it over the extended leg, using the arm on the side of the extended leg to gently pull the bent knee down toward the ground, keeping both shoulders flat until a stretch is felt.

Upper Body: Because trail runners tend to use their arms more than road runners, due to the need for balance and occasional trail touchdowns or scrambling, it is more important to keep your arms loose. The same goes for a trail runner's neck and shoulders. Long ascents or

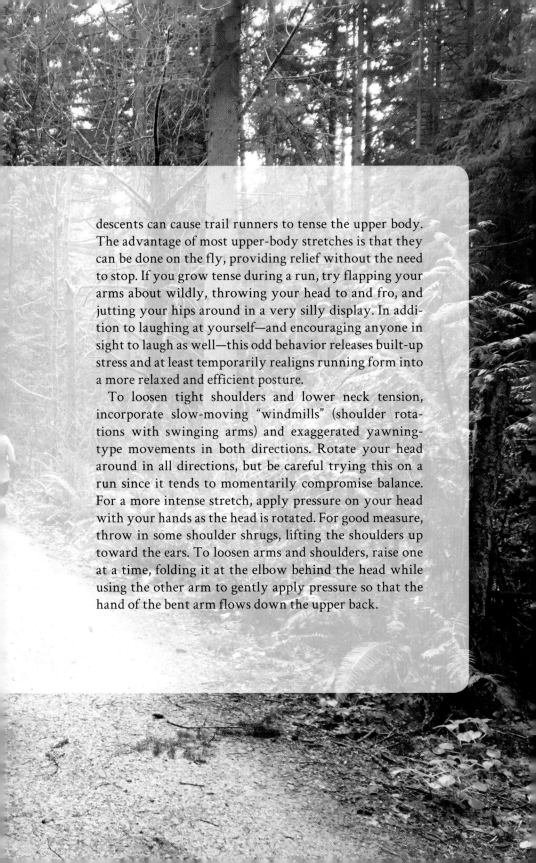

descents can cause trail runners to tense the upper body. The advantage of most upper-body stretches is that they can be done on the fly, providing relief without the need to stop. If you grow tense during a run, try flapping your arms about wildly, throwing your head to and fro, and jutting your hips around in a very silly display. In addition to laughing at yourself—and encouraging anyone in sight to laugh as well—this odd behavior releases built-up stress and at least temporarily realigns running form into a more relaxed and efficient posture.

To loosen tight shoulders and lower neck tension, incorporate slow-moving "windmills" (shoulder rotations with swinging arms) and exaggerated yawning-type movements in both directions. Rotate your head around in all directions, but be careful trying this on a run since it tends to momentarily compromise balance. For a more intense stretch, apply pressure on your head with your hands as the head is rotated. For good measure, throw in some shoulder shrugs, lifting the shoulders up toward the ears. To loosen arms and shoulders, raise one at a time, folding it at the elbow behind the head while using the other arm to gently apply pressure so that the hand of the bent arm flows down the upper back.

NORTH BEND–
RATTLESNAKE LEDGE

THE RUN DOWN

START: In the trailhead parking lot near I-90 exit 32; elevation 1,280 feet

OVERALL DISTANCE: 4 miles out and back

APPROXIMATE RUNNING TIME: 60 minutes

DIFFICULTY: Blue, with some elevation gain

ELEVATION GAIN: 967 feet

BEST SEASON TO RUN: Year-round; the trails absorb moisture well and have well-engineered runoff

DOG FRIENDLY: Leashed dogs permitted

PARKING: Free

OTHER USERS: None

CELL PHONE COVERAGE: Good

MORE INFORMATION: www.seattle.gov/Util/EnvironmentConservation/Education/CedarRiverWatershed/RattlesnakeLedge/index.htm

Rattlesnake Ledge.
PHOTO BY NANCY HOBBS

RATTLESNAKE LEDGE

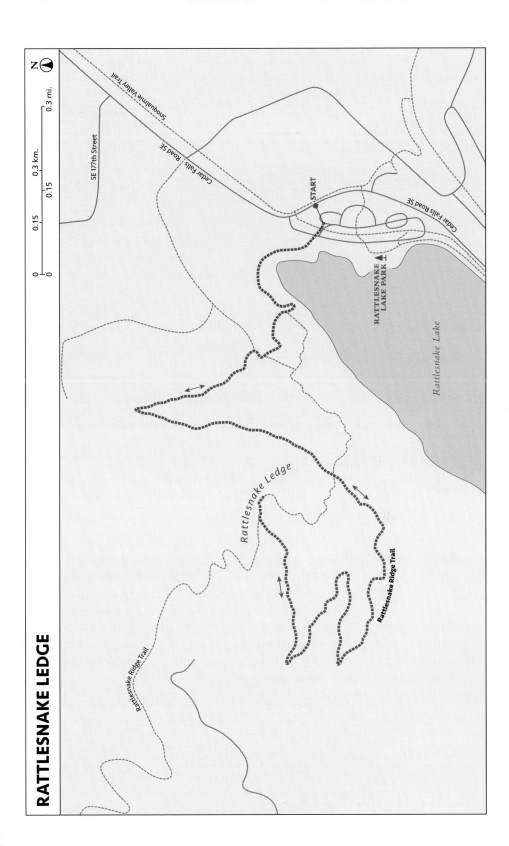

Rattlesnake Ledge.
PHOTO BY NANCY HOBBS

FINDING THE TRAILHEAD

From Seattle, follow I-90 east to 436th Avenue SE in Riverbend (exit 32). Follow to Cedar Falls Road. There is ample parking in the lot as well as parking on adjacent Cedar Falls Road.

RUN DESCRIPTION

The first 0.2 mile is on a flat, wide, gravel pathway, and the remainder of the trail is comprised of mostly doubletrack with long, loping switchbacks. Much of the route is within the forest. The footing is very good, although there are short sections laden with tree roots and rocks. This is a highly trafficked route due to its proximity to the city and the fantastic views afforded at the summit. This trail also connects with the 2.4-mile East Peak Trail and the 8.3-mile Snoqualmie Point Trail.

REDMOND WATERSHED PRESERVE

WITH 800 ACRES AND 7.5 MILES OF TRAILS, the Redmond Watershed Preserve offers wonderful trail-running opportunities through forest terrain, with gentle ascents and descents, twists and turns, switchbacks, and some exposed roots and rocks.

Redmond Watershed.
PHOTO BY NANCY HOBBS

5-MILE KEYHOLE LOOP

THE RUN DOWN

START: On the Trillium Trail near the outbuilding; elevation 482 feet

OVERALL DISTANCE: 4.7-mile keyhole

APPROXIMATE RUNNING TIME: 45 minutes

DIFFICULTY: Blue

ELEVATION GAIN: 301 feet

BEST SEASON TO RUN: Year-round

DOG FRIENDLY: No dogs

PARKING: Free parking in two lots (40+ spots) near the trailhead

OTHER USERS: Equestrians, mountain bikers on designated trails

CELL PHONE COVERAGE: Very good

MORE INFORMATION: www .redmond.gov/cms/one .aspx?portalId=169&page =4175

FINDING THE TRAILHEAD

Located at 21760 NE Novelty Hill Road in Redmond, a 0.25-mile drive from the main road greets users with a lovely pond and ample parking facilities near two trailheads.

RUN DESCRIPTION

For this keyhole-style loop, use the trailhead nearest the outbuilding, and head north on the Trillium Trail. Wide enough for four abreast in most spots, this is a nontechnical trail with some switchbacks and minimal climbing. The trail underfoot is soft and cushioned from the abundance of mulchy byproducts that fall from the coniferous trees. Entirely in the forest, there are no view corridors on this trail, although there is abundant greenery from ferns, mossy undergrowth, and pine needles.

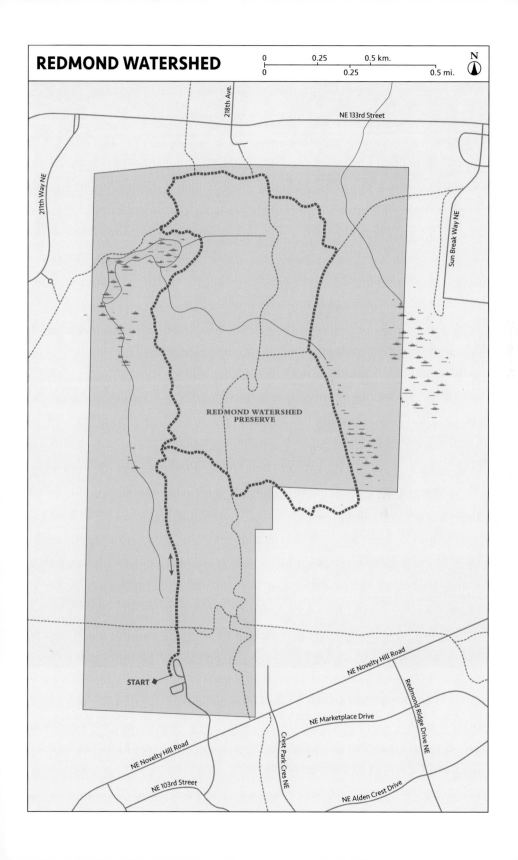

REDMOND WATERSHED

0   0.25   0.5 km.

0   0.25   0.5 mi.

N

218th Ave.

NE 133rd Street

211th Way NE

Sun Break Way NE

REDMOND WATERSHED
PRESERVE

START

NE Novelty Hill Road

Redmond Ridge Drive NE

NE Marketplace Drive

Crest Park Cres NE

NE Novelty Hill Road

NE 103rd Street

NE Alden Crest Drive

Redmond Watershed.
PHOTO BY NANCY HOBBS

This is an easy, enjoyable loop. Because the trails are mostly under forested canopy, there is a mulch base, which makes for an almost bouncy running sensation and enhances rain absorption. There will be an errant puddle or two along with some muddy sections after heavy rains, but consider this area as accessible year-round.

BRIDLE TRAILS STATE PARK

THIS URBAN-STYLE PARK IS LOCATED BETWEEN KIRKLAND AND BELLEVUE, Washington, with the main entrance in Kirkland. The park is in close proximity to neighborhoods that wrap around the outer circumference. There are three marked trail loops of varying distance, from 1 to 3.5 miles long.

LOOP RUN

THE RUN DOWN

START: The west end of the parking lot on 116th Ave. NE in Kirkland; elevation 488 feet

OVERALL DISTANCE: 3.5-mile loop

APPROXIMATE RUNNING TIME: 40 minutes

DIFFICULTY: Green

ELEVATION GAIN: 147 feet

BEST SEASON TO RUN: Year-round

DOG FRIENDLY: Leashed dogs permitted

PARKING: A day-use fee is charged; an annual Discover Pass is also available, allowing entrance to all Washington state parks. Ample parking is available.

OTHER USERS: Many equestrians, no cyclists

CELL PHONE COVERAGE: Very good

MORE INFORMATION: www .bridletrails.org/about_the_ park/park_information.html

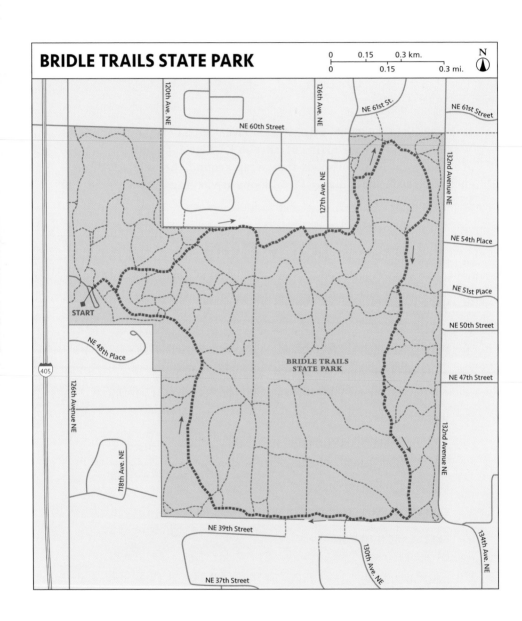

BRIDLE TRAILS STATE PARK

0   0.15   0.3 km.

0   0.15   0.3 mi.

N

120th Ave. NE

NE 60th Street

126th Ave. NE

127th Ave. NE

NE 61st St.

NE 61st Street

132nd Avenue NE

NE 54th Place

NE 51st Place

NE 50th Street

NE 47th Street

START

NE 48th Place

405

126th Avenue NE

118th Ave. NE

BRIDLE TRAILS
STATE PARK

132nd Avenue NE

NE 39th Street

130th Ave. NE

134th Ave. NE

NE 37th Street

Bridle Trails State Park.
PHOTO BY NANCY HOBBS

FINDING THE TRAILHEAD

From Seattle, follow WA 520 E to Northrup Way in Bellevue. Take 116th Avenue N to the parking lot at 5300 116th Avenue NE in Kirkland. The trailhead is on the west end of the parking lot.

RUN DESCRIPTION

Follow the marked signs with a paw print for the Coyote Trail, running the loop in a clockwise direction. When there is a questionable connection or junction, take the trail to the right. The trail is mostly under forested canopies on doubletrack, and there are sections of singletrack with slight elevation changes. The forest canopy makes for a soft trail that, for the most part, stays puddle- and mud-free, other than sloppy sections you'll find after heavy rains. You should consider this area accessible year-round.

WHAT TO WEAR ON THE TRAIL

TRAIL RUNNERS OFTEN FACE THE DIFFICULT "WHAT AM I GOING TO WEAR?" dilemma when they look out the window before a run and try to foresee any temperature changes and anticipate their needs. Layering is a compelling solution to that problem. With different layers of apparel, a trail runner can adjust during the run to moderate temperature, both in response to internal changes in exertion and to external changes in weather. Technologically advanced fabrics have put a new twist to layering, elevating it to a modern art form, the object of which is to find the perfect balance of performance, temperature regulation, moisture control, insulation, and protection from exogenous elements such as wind, snow, and rain.

Layers can be broken into three primary categories: base (against the skin), mid (also known as the insulating, thermal, or performance layer), and outer (shell). While the following discussion is divided into these three categories, keep in mind that several manufacturers, mostly in the outdoor industry, have designed excellent pieces of apparel that blur the layering distinctions by incorporating two or even all three layers into a single garment.

BASE LAYERS AND SOCKS

Worn next to your skin, base layers tend to be soft and are primarily designed to wick moisture from the skin while providing some warmth. Cotton, once very popular among runners as a base layer, is somewhat extinct as a performance fabric and is not recommended as a base layer because it retains moisture, does not breathe well, and becomes abrasive to skin when wet. In contrast, modern merino wool—which does not itch—is an ideal base layer material because it maintains dryness, helps regulate body temperature, and is resistant to bacteria.

The importance of an effective base layer must not be overlooked: A trail runner can wear the most advanced shell on the market and it will be worthless if the runner is soaking wet on the inside.

Although a fabric's moisture management ability is important, the first priority in a base layer should be the material's ability to help regulate the body's microclimate. Ideally, a base layer maintains a sufficiently warm or cool temperature so that the runner is neither shivering nor sweating. By avoiding overheating, a runner will release less moisture, which helps to maintain better hydration and performance. Nonetheless, since perspiration is a natural component of exertion, an effective base layer regulates the body's microclimate by wicking moisture away from the skin so that it can evaporate or be passed through mid and outer layers.

Base layer fabrics wick moisture through one or a combination of chemical or mechanical techniques. Most technical synthetic base layer fabrics are known as "hydrophobic," which means they repel moisture instead of absorbing it. Polyester, nylon, and polypropylene are the most common hydrophobic fabrics used to draw moisture from the skin and repel it outward, where it evaporates if exposed to the air, or transfers to a mid or outer layer, where it can be dispersed.

Base layers should be somewhat form-fitting or tight. Some moisture-wicking fabrics work best if they are snug against the skin. That contact allows them to wick moisture at an early stage. Some fabrics are even able to transport moisture while it is in the vapor state. Base layers should fit well with the trail runner's particular body type; and if chafing is a concern, select pieces that use flat seam construction.

When it comes to running in the cold, trail runners can keep their legs warm by choosing between tights and "loose tights" (also called "relaxed-fit pants" or "track pants"), all of which are made from wicking base layer fabrics with Lycra, Spandex, or other resilient materials blended in to make them soft, flexible, and quite warm. When it is really cold, double-layer tights, tights with windproof panels, or wind pants over tights usually keep the legs adequately warm. Whether wearing shorts, tights, or pants, consider wearing a base layer of Lycra, Spandex, wind briefs, or wind shorts that feature strategically placed front microfiber panels to protect the more sensitive parts of the anatomy from chilling winds. Wearing fuller-cut undershorts as a base layer under tights or running shorts will also reduce inner-thigh chafe. Compression tights, due to their constriction of blood flow, may not have the desired thermal qualities of looser-fitting leggings.

Regardless of aesthetic preferences, the most important qualities in choosing socks for trail running are temperature regulation, moisture management, cushioning, and protection from blisters. Some trail runners prefer thin synthetic socks that have minimal cushioning and offer a better trail "feel." Others find that thicker wool socks maintain a comfortable foot temperature in varying weather, in wet conditions, or on trail runs with water crossings. Those concerned about cushioning may opt for socks that are constructed with various weave patterns in different zones of the footbed to enhance cushioning and comfort. Some trail runners use trail shoes that feature relatively firm midsoles and temper that rigidity with cushioned socks.

MID LAYER

The second layer, known as the mid, thermal, or performance layer, is a continuation of the base layer in managing moisture. However, the mid layer also provides thermal insulation. Mid layers work with the base layer to transfer moisture to the outer layer and are often made of the same hydrophobic materials, but with a more spacious weave. Fleece, especially microfiber fleece, works well as a mid layer because it has moisture-transfer qualities, boasts a high warmth-to-weight ratio, and is not bulky. Some thermal layer fabrics use quilted weaves or other patterns that incorporate air pockets for increased warmth.

OUTERWEAR

Finding an ideal outer layer or shell presents the problem of balancing and achieving both breathability and weather resistance. With the goal of keeping you warm and dry by resisting or blocking the elements, such as wind, rain, or snow, the shell must also allow perspiration to escape through vents and technical features of the fabric. Except under extreme conditions, totally waterproof fabrics are overkill and even undesirable for trail runners. Waterproof materials tend to add bulk, inflexibility, expense, and especially reduced breathability to the garment. A stormproof outer layer sounds great for trail runners who confront freezing rain; but if their jackets and pants do not breathe well, those runners quickly become as wet from the inside as they would have had they chosen shells that lacked any water-resistant properties.

In most conditions, trail runners will be served best by microfiber outer layers that allow molecules of body-temperature vapor to escape while being windproof and water resistant rather than waterproof. Microfiber garments are often less expensive, weigh less, pack smaller, and are more pliant and therefore less noisy than their waterproof counterparts. Some manufacturers have applied laminates or encapsulating processes to enhance the windproof qualities and water-resisting performance of microfiber apparel.

Important qualities that distinguish functional trail-running shells from those that are better used for other types of outdoor recreation include the presence and optimum placement of venting systems, pockets, hoods, cuffs, closures, lining, and abrasion-resistant panels. When considering the purchase of a jacket with all the bells and whistles, think about whether the weight and cost of each zippered, snapped, Velcroed, or cord-locked opening is necessary.

Decide what style of shell—pullover "shirts," full-zip jackets, or vests—is best. Also consider the costs and benefits of such features as self-storage pockets and the integration of other fabrics in various panels, such as fleece, stretch material, breathable material, wicking material, or mesh back sections. If night running with motor vehicles is part of the regime, reflective taping is a worthwhile feature. Finally, try on the jacket to check the collar height, and look for the presence of a fleece chin cover to protect you from exposure to or abrasion from cold zipper pulls.

Head and Hands

Trail runners should think twice before setting out on a jaunt without a hat or cap. Caps, especially those with bills, protect the scalp and eyes from sun and reduce the chances of overheating. Many caps are made out of moisture-wicking materials, and some feature mesh sides for venting heat. Some hats are made specifically for blocking the sun, having been constructed of fabric with a high SPF rating, and feature draped flaps that shield the neck from sunrays.

Given that approximately half the body's heat escapes through the head, hats are the single most important item of apparel for maintaining warmth. Many hats can be rolled up or down to expose or cover ears as a means of adjusting for a more comfortable temperature. When running in extreme cold, look for hats that are made with fleece, wind-blocking materials, wool, or a combination of fabrics that preserve warmth yet wick away perspiration under a variety of foul weather conditions. When the temperature is particularly frigid or if the windchill factor makes exposure and frostbite a real danger, it may be necessary to run with a face covering, neck gaiter, or balaclava to protect skin.

Mittens are much warmer than gloves; and if manual dexterity is not a concern, mittens are probably a better choice for colder climes. Some trail runners wear bicycling or weightlifting gloves with padded palms to protect their hand from falls or when scrambling.

Gloves and mittens are made in a variety of different fabrics and vary in thickness. Some are made of moisture-wicking, windproof, or waterproof fabrics, while others feature high-tech materials that are either integrated into or coat glove or mitten linings to maintain a comfortable temperature. If the hand temperature rises above the engineered comfort zone or "target" temperature, the material absorbs the heat and stores it for subsequent release should the hands cool below the target temperature. As a final consideration, if the backs of mittens or gloves are likely to be used as a nose wipe, make sure the fabric is soft.

LORD HILL REGIONAL PARK

THIS PARK PACKS A PUNCH, with over 6 miles of trails that meander in and out of forest, meadows, and wetlands throughout 1,436 acres. The Snohomish River flows along the southwest side of the park, and the higher points provide panoramic views of the Snohomish Valley and the Cascade and Olympic mountain ranges. Carry a map to assist in navigating the trails, which are not very well marked. A parking lot is located on the north side of the park at 150th Street SE, providing access to the northern and western tier trails, which connect to those on the south and east. Trails can also be accessed from the south off Old Tester Road, but only on-street parking is available unless there is a special event, in which case the gate leading to a parking lot is open.

5.8-MILE LOOP

THE RUN DOWN

START: River Quarry Rd. off Old Tester Rd. in Snohomish; elevation 34 feet

OVERALL DISTANCE: 5.8-mile loop

APPROXIMATE RUNNING TIME: 60 minutes

DIFFICULTY: Blue

ELEVATION GAIN: 988 feet

BEST SEASON TO RUN: Year-round

DOG FRIENDLY: Leashed dogs permitted

PARKING: Free

OTHER USERS: Equestrians and mountain bikers

CELL PHONE COVERAGE: Good

MORE INFORMATION: snohomishcountywa.gov/ Facilities/Facility/Details/ Lord-Hill-Regional-Park-35

Lord Hill Regional Park - 5.8-Mile.
PHOTO BY NANCY HOBBS

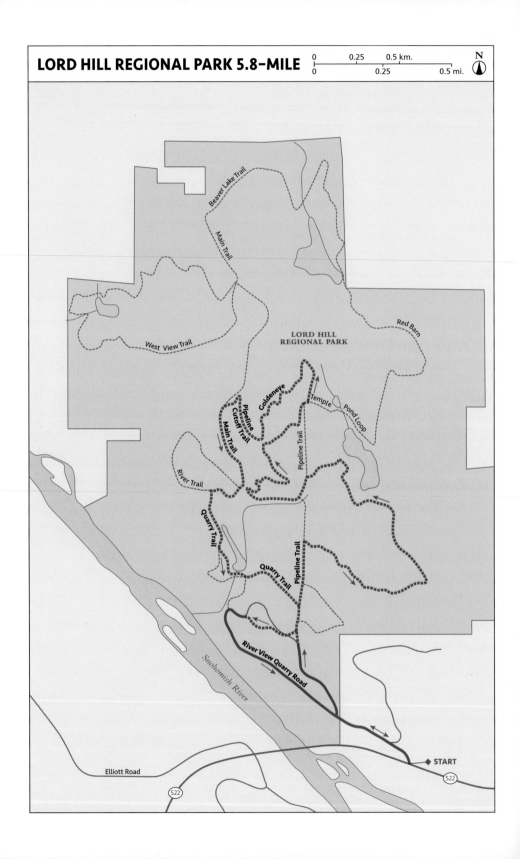

LORD HILL REGIONAL PARK 5.8-MILE

| 0 | 0.25 | 0.5 km. |
| 0 | 0.25 | 0.5 mi. |

N

Beaver Lake Trail

Main Trail

West View Trail

LORD HILL
REGIONAL PARK

Red Barn

Goldeneye

Pipeline Cutoff Trail

Main Trail

Temple

Pond Loop

Pipeline Trail

River Trail

Quarry Trail

Pipeline Trail

Quarry Trail

River View Quarry Road

Snohomish River

Elliott Road

522

START

522

FINDING THE TRAILHEAD

From Bellevue, follow 405 N to WA 522 E. Follow Tester Road to Old Tester Road. Start from the south side of the park off Old Tester Road. After parking on the street, head north on River Quarry Road to start the run. There are no restrooms at this entry point to the park.

RUN DESCRIPTION

This loop route starts on a mixed roadbed of pavement and gravel and heads uphill to the Pipeline Trail, accessed by turning right on a double-wide trail through a meadow. Look up and start a climb, which has grades up to 38 percent. Although not very long, this initial ascent is a grunt.

Head right into the forest after the climb, and continue on a counter-clockwise route with some ascending and descending and numerous twists and turns over occasional rooted and muddy sections. These short and quick, motion-sickness-inducing turns create a challenge, especially in conjunction with tricky footing that requires sharp focus to stay upright. There are a few sections through open meadows, some long stretches down a fire road, and areas through overgrown weeds, which sometimes require quick maneuvering and high steps along the singletrack trails. This is trail running, after all.

EAST OF SEATTLE

8.8-MILE TOUR OF THE PARK

THE RUN DOWN

START: River Quarry Rd. off Old Tester Rd. in Snohomish; elevation 89 feet

OVERALL DISTANCE: 8.8-mile loop run counterclockwise

APPROXIMATE RUNNING TIME: 90 minutes

DIFFICULTY: Blue

ELEVATION GAIN: 1,407 feet

BEST SEASON TO RUN: Year-round

DOG FRIENDLY: Leashed dogs permitted

PARKING: Free

OTHER USERS: Mountain bikers, equestrians

CELL PHONE COVERAGE: Good

MORE INFORMATION: snohomishcountywa.gov/ Facilities/Facility/Details/ Lord-Hill-Regional-Park-35

FINDING THE TRAILHEAD

From Bellevue, follow 405 N to WA 522 E. Follow Tester Road to Old Tester Road. Start from the south side of the park off Old Tester Road. After parking on the street, head north on River Quarry Road to start the run. There are no restrooms at this entry point to the park.

RUN DESCRIPTION

Start on the River View Quarry Road heading north and follow to the Pipeline Trail. Continue on the Temple Pond Loop and connect with the Red Barn Trail north to Easy 8 at approximately 3 miles into the route. A short stint on the Pipeline Trail leads to Beaver Lake Trail and then sections on the Upper Springboard Trail and the Loop Trail on the far west side of the park. The Main Trail and River Trail Cutoff lead back to the River Quarry Trail and a return to the parking lot.

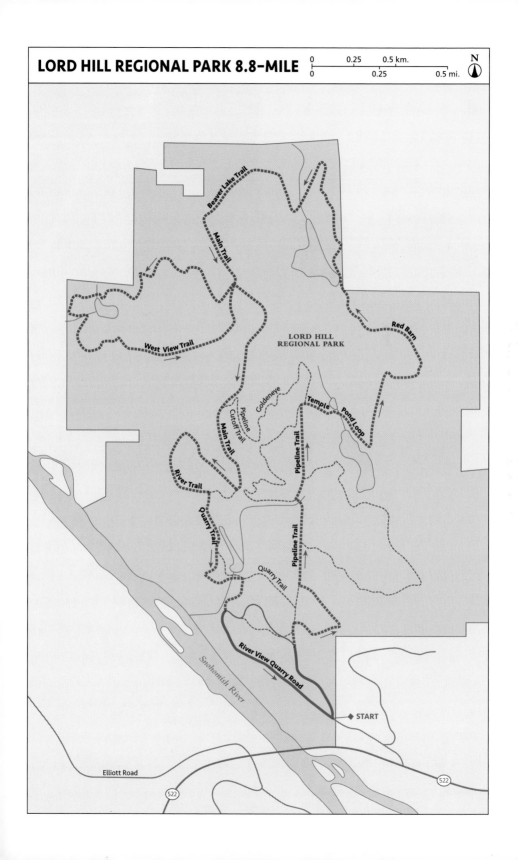

LORD HILL REGIONAL PARK 8.8-MILE

0   0.25   0.5 km.
0   0.25   0.5 mi.

N

Beaver Lake Trail

Main Trail

West View Trail

Red Barn

LORD HILL
REGIONAL PARK

Goldeneye

Temple

Pond Loop

Pipeline
Cutoff Trail

Main Trail

Pipeline Trail

River Trail

Quarry Trail

Quarry Trail

Pipeline Trail

River View Quarry Road

Snohomish River

♦ START

Elliott Road

522

522

3-MILE LOOP FROM THE NORTH END

THE RUN DOWN

START: Trailhead at 12921 150th St. SE in Snohomish; elevation 550 feet

OVERALL DISTANCE: 3-mile loop

APPROXIMATE RUNNING TIME: 30 minutes

DIFFICULTY: Green

ELEVATION GAIN: 381 feet

BEST SEASON TO RUN: Year-round

DOG FRIENDLY: Leashed dogs permitted

PARKING: Free

OTHER USERS: Mountain bikers, equestrians

CELL PHONE COVERAGE: Good

MORE INFORMATION: snohomishcountywa.gov/ Facilities/Facility/Details/ Lord-Hill-Regional-Park-35

FINDING THE TRAILHEAD

From Seattle, head north on I-5 to WA 520 E. Continue to 405 N to 522 E to W Main Street. Follow Old Snohomish Monroe to 127th Avenue SE. Turn left on 150th Street. Park at the north end of the park, at 12921 150th Street SE in Snohomish, accessed from Old Snohomish Monroe Road as described above.

RUN DESCRIPTION

From the trailhead, follow the boardwalk to the Beaver Lake Trail, which connects south with the Pipeline Trail. Continue to the Pipeline Cutoff Trail, and return on the Main Trail for this enjoyable loop.

Some of the intersections are not well marked, and much of the route is in the forest. Muddy spots and frequent horse droppings are common, and it is especially muddy in rainy periods. This is an easy introduction to trail running, as there is nothing technical about the loop.

Running Gear

Eyewear

RUNNING EYEWEAR HAS PROGRESSED ENORMOUSLY IN THE LAST DECADE, to the point that sunglasses are now functional and extremely protective (as well as looking pretty cool). Because trail runners constantly use their eyes to scope out their next steps and enjoy the awesome views, the eyes are very valuable assets—and worth preserving. With lighter frames, full protection from harmful ultraviolet rays and lenses that shield eyes from insects, dirt, and shrubbery, modern glasses are worth wearing. Even on cloudy days or in partially forested areas, a pair of sunglasses is a good addition to your gear. Lighter colored or photochromic lenses that darken when exposed to brighter light may be used, and it is easy to place the glasses atop your head when you don't need the full-on protection of the lenses.

Today's eyewear also tends to be versatile, sporting features such as adjustable bridges and temples and interchangeable lenses to accommodate changes in brightness. Some sports glasses have venting features that prevent lenses from fogging. Other attributes to consider include rubberized bridges to prevent slipping and straight or wraparound frames that relieve temple pressure. Photochromic lenses are particularly well suited for trails because they adjust to the lighting, getting darker when exposed to more sun and lighter (even clear) when in the shade or the dark.

When shopping for trail-running eyewear, look for lenses that offer full UV protection. Sports eyewear prices range dramatically. Make sure the glasses have the features that are most desirable—lightweight, fit, UV protection, and high resolution—before buying a pair of cheap gas station glasses or investing a week's wages in some designer shades.

ELECTRONICS

Although trail runners are better known for their back-to-nature approach and avoiding modern technological devices—especially when compared to road runners, mountain bikers, or triathletes (aka "tri-geeks")—certain gadgets add to the trail-running experience and can be used discreetly or, in some cases, rather boldly, as when shared on social media. A cell phone carried in a hydration pack can be a lifesaver in the event of an emergency, as is the case with a satellite phone or tracker device.

Watches have come a long way since the days of just telling the time of day and perhaps the date. Now they are "wrist-top computers" or "action trackers," capable of telling distance traveled, speed, leg speed cadence, direction, barometric pressure, weather trends, altitude, heart rate, ascent and descent rates; and they can even receive and transmit messages. Whether knowing any of that data is desirable is a subjective question, but some of it can be quite motivational, assist coaches, and make trail runners safer. Trail runners are now able to explore new terrain with fewer worries of getting hopelessly lost or being hit by an unexpected storm. Neither will we have an excuse for being late.

Flashlights and headlamps are important devices for trail runners who run in the dark, especially ultradistance runners who are likely to race or train at night. Many types of flashlights and headlamps are on the market, so weigh anticipated needs against the different attributes of various light sources. A flashlight provides precise directional focus, but usually requires one hand to hold it. In contrast, headlamps free the hands, but some runners find the light angle makes it difficult to discern trail obstacles because it shines from above.

Flashlights and headlamps come in different weights, brightnesses, and with a variety of light sources, such as halogen, fluorescent, LED (light-emitting diodes), and conventional and somewhat outdated tungsten bulb lights. These different types of light vary in brightness, energy efficiency, durability, and cost. Some units allow for adjustability in brightness and intensity of focus, while others come with rechargeable battery packs and water-resistant or waterproof qualities.

Miscellaneous Gear

Thanks to the influence of Nordic skiers, adventure racers, and European trail runners, the use of lightweight trekking poles has increased. Runners use these collapsible poles to help redistribute the workload from their legs to the upper body, especially on ascents. Poles also help with balance. They should be light, sturdy, and easy to carry when not in use. If the poles have baskets, they should be minimal in size to avoid entanglements with brush, trees, and rocks and reduce awkwardness in use. While sharp points make the poles excellent spears for charging beasts, they can also do a fine job on your own feet.

Trail runners should also consider wearing low-cut gaiters, even when there is no snow around. Gaiters prevent gravel, scree, sand, stones, and dirt from penetrating the ankle collar of shoes, thus relieving trail runners from the frustration of running with a buildup of trail debris at the bottom of their shoes or the annoyance of having to stop to remove the offending substance from shoe and sock. Some trail shoes are now designed with gaiter attachments or snug-fitting ankle collars to prevent any intrusion of debris.

From the safety perspective, trail runners may consider carrying a first aid kit, snakebite kit, or other basic backcountry safety items like a lighter, about 20 feet of lightweight rope, and a Swiss army knife, Leatherman, or other multipurpose tool. Maps are also very useful. It might also be wise to pack a whistle or mace to repel uninvited advances, whether animal or human. Consider bringing duct tape—the universal solution, panacea, and fix-all that works in a pinch as a make-shift gaiter, blister preventer or mender, cut patcher, splint, tourniquet, garment rip stopper, etc. In sum, if a trail emergency can't be remedied with duct tape, it's time for grave concern.

For those who run with canine companions, some of the leashes on the market make life a lot easier. There are "hands-free" leashes that are worn around the waist and attach to the dog's collar via quick-release mechanisms for safety and convenience. Other leashes are made from elastic shock-cord to allow some play without excessive slack, a real convenience when trails are rocky or otherwise require quick maneuvers that may not coincide with movements of the dog.

Another handy item is a leash pack, which conveniently slides over a leash to carry "poop bags," both empty and full. Collapsible lightweight bowls that pack onto a leash or into a fanny pack make it easy to keep four-legged trail runners well hydrated and fed on the run.

PARADISE VALLEY
CONSERVATION AREA

WITH 13 MILES OF DESIGNATED TRAILS WITHIN THIS 793-ACRE PARK, there is terrain for all levels and abilities. The park offers a mixture of multiuse trails, foot-traffic-only trails, one-way routes, and double- and singletrack terrain in and out of the forest. The trails in this area are very well signed and marked, leaving no doubt you're on the chosen route. Even if the parking lot is full, the trails are not crowded because there are so many different options from which to choose.

Paradise Valley Conservation Area.
PHOTO BY NANCY HOBBS

3.4-MILE LOOP

THE RUN DOWN

START: Trailhead on the north side of the Paradise Valley parking lot; elevation 336 feet

OVERALL DISTANCE: 3.4-mile loop

APPROXIMATE RUNNING TIME: 40 minutes

DIFFICULTY: Green

ELEVATION GAIN: 156 feet

BEST SEASON TO RUN: Year-round

DOG FRIENDLY: Leashed dogs permitted

PARKING: Free

OTHER USERS: Equestrians and mountain bikers on designated trails

CELL PHONE COVERAGE: Good

MORE INFORMATION: snohomishcountywa.gov/ Facilities/Facility/Details/ Paradise-Valley-Conservation-Area-PVCA-66

FINDING THE TRAILHEAD

From Seattle take I-5 North to WA 520 E. Connect to I-405 N to WA 522 E to Paradise Lake Road. Enjoy a leisurely drive along the rural two-lane Paradise Lake Road, which leads to a signed parking lot. The trailhead is on the north side of the lot. There are no restrooms.

RUN DESCRIPTION

Start on the doubletrack Mainline Trail for this loop run through the forest encompassing three additional trails: the Red Alder, the 106 Drive, and the Cascara. The Red Alder is singletrack, complete with exposed roots and rocks and some quick and sharp race-car-like turns. Occasional sunlight peeks through the trees above. The 106 Drive Trail, which joins up with the Cascara Trail, is also singletrack.

With just slight elevation gain, this route is great for trail runners of all levels. There are a few low-lying sections, which can be muddy, but the design of the trails provides a few V sections to redirect traffic to a slightly higher spot on the trail to stay dry. This route provides a rather quiet and serene experience, with just a bit of traffic noise from the nearby Paradise Lake Road on a portion of the Cascara Trail.

PARADISE VALLEY CONSERVATION AREA

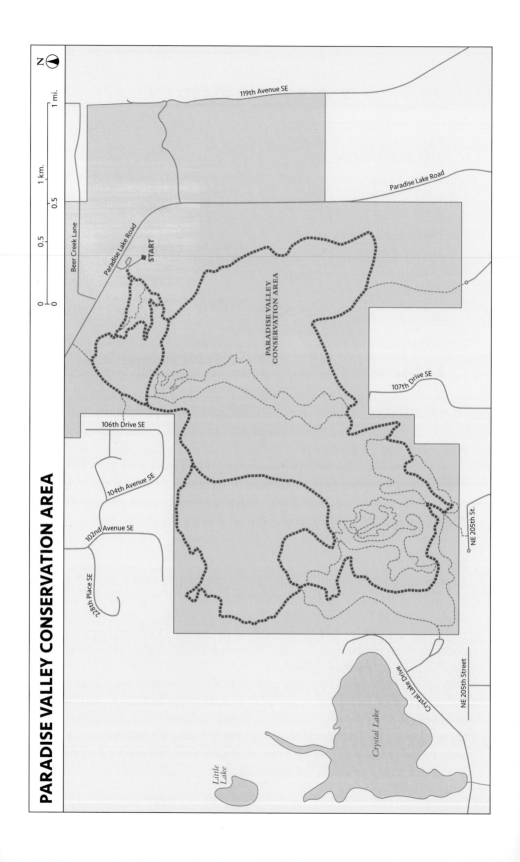

4.4-MILE LOOP

THE RUN DOWN

START: Trailhead on the north side of the Paradise Valley parking lot; elevation 420 feet

OVERALL DISTANCE: 4.4-mile loop

APPROXIMATE RUNNING TIME: 45 minutes

DIFFICULTY: Green

ELEVATION GAIN: 367 feet

BEST SEASON TO RUN: Year-round

DOG FRIENDLY: Leashed dogs permitted

PARKING: Free

OTHER USERS: Mountain bikers and equestrians on designated trails

CELL PHONE COVERAGE: Good

MORE INFORMATION: snohomishcountywa.gov/Facilities/Facility/Details/Paradise-Valley-Conservation-Area-PVCA-66

FINDING THE TRAILHEAD

 Take Paradise Lake Road to the signed parking lot. The trailhead is on the north side of the lot. There are no restrooms.

APPAREL EDGE

Dressing properly—especially for running in the extreme weather conditions we often see in Seattle—has become a science of its own. Trail runners must choose garments with care. An error in clothing selection can ruin what would otherwise be a trail adventure in exciting weather and may have far more deleterious effects. The wrong mix of clothes can result in overheating and dehydration or, conversely, in chilled muscles and even hypothermia. Fortunately, with today's high-tech fabrics, even the newest trail runner finds it easy to dress for success and enjoy the experience in varying weather conditions. And although modern textiles have come a long way, some of the old basics still rule. Wool remains one of the best all-around fabrics because of its wicking, thermal, antimicrobial, and resilient qualities, especially in merino, its new washable and itch-free version.

Paradise Valley
Conservation Area.
PHOTO BY NANCY HOBBS

RUN DESCRIPTION

Start on the Mainline Trail heading south turning at the first fork to the left on the Woodland Plateau Trail. After less than 1 mile, head east on the Southern Traverse Trail. Just beyond 2 miles and a short stint on the Mainline Trail to the Two Trees Trail. Reach the Ephemeral Trail at about the 2¼-mile point and continue to the Red Alder Trail. At roughly 3.5 miles, it's back on the Mainline Trail for a short segment to the Cascara Trail leading back to the Whispering Firs Trail and the parking lot start point. This perimeter loop provides a wonderful overview of the park environs. The route is on singletrack trail, most of which is forested, with a fair amount of twists and turns and roots and rocks. The trail signage is very good, but carrying a map will assist in navigation at junctions to ensure you stay on our intended route.

COUGAR MOUNTAIN

ESTABLISHED IN 1985, COUGAR MOUNTAIN REGIONAL WILDLAND PARK is in King County, Washington, near the towns of Bellevue and Issaquah. A gem in the region, there are 38 miles of trails accessible from four major trailhead locations within the 3,115-acre park, from which you can start an adventure ranging in length from 30 minutes to an all-day excursion. The park is connected to Squak Mountain State Park by the Cougar-Squak Corridor, which together create a protected area of public land of approximately 5,000 acres. The terrain covers a mix of singletrack, wider, forested paths, and fire roads. There are footbridges, switchbacks, ascents, descents, and rolling terrain, along with view corridors in the upper reaches of the park. The park's address is 18201 SE Cougar Mountain Drive, Bellevue, WA 98059.

The park's four trailheads are listed below:

1. Jim Whittaker Wilderness Peak Trailhead (SR 900/Renton-Issaquah Road SE, 3.3 miles south of I-90): This small parking area provides access to the trail system on the east side of the park via the Whittaker Wilderness Peak Trail. No equestrians or bikes at this location.

2. Anti-Aircraft Peak Trailhead (SE Cougar Mountain Drive): This area is located close to the top of Cougar Mountain and provides wonderful views to the north (sometimes you can catch a glimpse of Mount Baker). Many of the wildland park's trails are accessed from this trailhead. No bikes are permitted at this trailhead.

3. Sky Country Trailhead (166th Way SE): Located near the former Nike missile site, no bikes are permitted here either.

4. Red Town Trailhead (Lakemont Boulevard SE/Newcastle Coal Creek Road): This trailhead provides quick access to many historical mining exhibits in the northwest sector of the park and also provides access to the adjacent Coal Creek Trail. And again, sucks to be a cyclist: No bikes allowed.

RED TOWN TRAILHEAD

THE RUN DOWN

START: Trailhead off Lakemont Blvd. SE; elevation 664 feet

OVERALL DISTANCE: 3.4-mile loop with out-and-back legs

APPROXIMATE RUNNING TIME: 40 minutes

DIFFICULTY: Blue

ELEVATION GAIN: 474 feet

BEST SEASON TO RUN: Year-round

DOG FRIENDLY: Leashed dogs permitted

PARKING: Free

OTHER USERS: Equestrians; no bikers

CELL PHONE COVERAGE: Good

MORE INFORMATION: ftp://ftp.kingcounty.gov/gis/Web/VMC/recreation/BCT_CougarMtn_brochure.pdf and http://www.kingcounty.gov/services/parks-recreation/parks/parks-and-natural-lands/popular-parks/cougar.aspx

FINDING THE TRAILHEAD

From Seattle, take I-90 E to exit 13 for Lakemont Boulevard SE. Park at the lot off Lakemont Boulevard SE. There is room for about twenty cars, and there is trail signage as well as portable toilets. Several trails start from this parking area.

RUN DESCRIPTION

After walking past the service gate, head to the lower trail on the right. It is signed as the wildside trail. The trail begins as doubletrack and changes to singletrack and includes some stairs and runs across a few footbridges. After about 0.7 mile, turn right toward the Leo Wall Trail. Follow that to a short out-and-back "lookout" that isn't really because you are embedded in thick forest.

Continue uphill to the Far Country Lookout for a second out-and-back. This lookout point is the real deal, and, on a clear day, there is a view to the

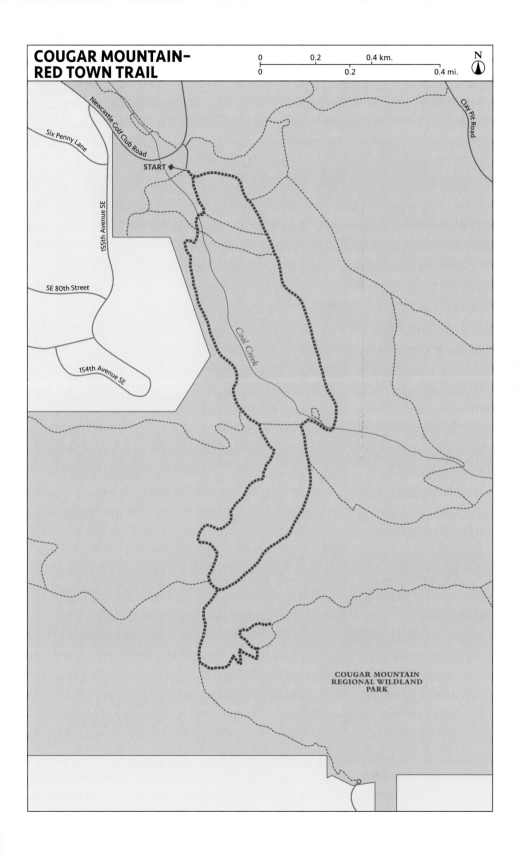

COUGAR MOUNTAIN–
RED TOWN TRAIL

0   0.2   0.4 km.
0   0.2   0.4 mi.

N

Six Penny Lane

Newcastle Golf Club Road

Clay Pit Road

155th Avenue SE

START

SE 80th Street

154th Avenue SE

Coal Creek

COUGAR MOUNTAIN
REGIONAL WILDLAND
PARK

Cougar Mountain - Red Town Trail.
PHOTO BY NANCY HOBBS

west toward Lake Washington. Return on the Indian Trail, connecting to the Red Town Trail for this counterclockwise loop.

The trails are well marked, but it is best to carry a map to better navigate your intended route. On the opposite side of Lakemont Boulevard SE, there are additional trail access points to the Coal Creek Nature Area.

SHANGRI LA

THE RUN DOWN

START: Anti-Aircraft Peak Trailhead; elevation 1,421 feet

OVERALL DISTANCE: 1.3-mile clockwise loop

APPROXIMATE RUNNING TIME: 15 minutes

DIFFICULTY: Green

ELEVATION GAIN: 199 feet

BEST SEASON TO RUN: Year-round; can be muddy in spots

DOG FRIENDLY: Leashed dogs permitted on trails

PARKING: Free

OTHER USERS: Equestrians on designated trails; mountain bikers.

CELL PHONE COVERAGE: Good

MORE INFORMATION: www .kingcounty.gov/services/ parks-recreation/parks/parks- and-natural-lands/popular- parks/cougar.aspx

FINDING THE TRAILHEAD

From Seattle, take I-90 E to Lakemont Boulevard SE (exit 13), and follow Lakemont Boulevard SE to to SE Cougar Mountain Drive. Begin at the Cougar Mountain Drive entrance.

RUN DESCRIPTION

From the Cougar Mountain Drive entrance at the Anti-Aircraft Peak Trailhead, visit the Pagoda overlook. Run on the Shangri La Trail.

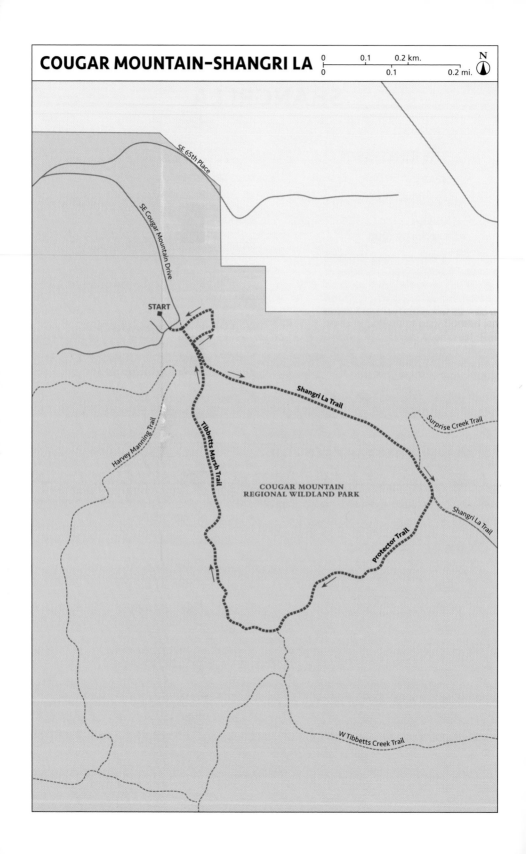

COUGAR MOUNTAIN–SHANGRI LA

0   0.1   0.2 km.
0   0.1   0.2 mi.

N

SE 65th Place

SE Cougar Mountain Drive

START

Shangri La Trail

Surprise Creek Trail

Harvey Manning Trail

Tibbetts Marsh Trail

COUGAR MOUNTAIN
REGIONAL WILDLAND PARK

protector Trail

Shangri La Trail

W Tibbetts Creek Trail

COAL CREEK TRAIL

THE RUN DOWN

START: Coal Creek Pkwy SE trailhead; elevation 183 feet

OVERALL DISTANCE: 5.1 miles out and back

APPROXIMATE RUNNING TIME: 60 minutes

DIFFICULTY: Green

ELEVATION GAIN: 452 feet

BEST SEASON TO RUN: Year-round, but trails can get muddy in heavy rains

DOG FRIENDLY: Leashed dogs permitted

PARKING: Free

OTHER USERS: Equestrians; no cyclists

CELL PHONE COVERAGE: Good

MORE INFORMATION: www .kingcounty.gov/services/ parks-recreation/parks/parks-and-natural-lands/popular-parks/cougar.aspx

FINDING THE TRAILHEAD

There are two access points, one to the east via the Red Town Trailhead (cross the street from the parking lot to start the trail heading west); the other from Coal Creek Parkway SE (via I-90). This mapped route starts from the west side heading east toward Red Town Trailhead.

RUN DESCRIPTION

Begin at the Coal Creek Parkway SE trailhead. After a short section on a wide, crushed gravel path, the treadway changes to a wide, hard-packed dirt trail, before narrowing further to singletrack trail. The majority of the trail is heavily forested and is flanked by Coal Creek, which is within earshot almost the entire route. Enjoy two waterfalls, cross several footbridges, ascend wooden steps, traverse switchbacks, return to some sections of crushed gravel, and reach the turnaround point at Red Town Trailhead after 2.5 miles.

On the return trip, you can take two deviations on side trails to experience other trails in the park. The first is the Interpretive Loop, on the left just 0.1 mile after the turnaround. This short loop crosses a footbridge and returns to the Coal Creek Trail in under 0.2 mile. The second is the

COUGAR MOUNTAIN–COAL CREEK TRAIL

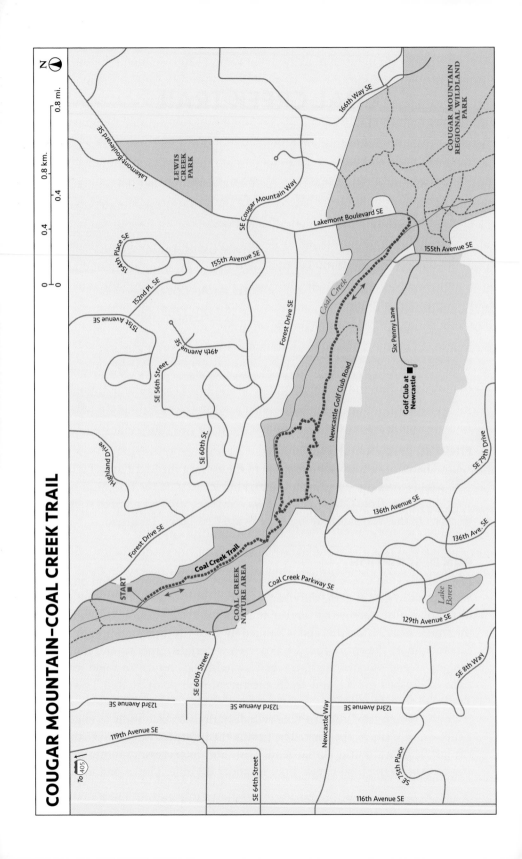

Cougar Mountain - Coal Creek Trail.
PHOTO BY NANCY HOBBS

Primrose Trail, to the right approximately 1 mile beyond. At just under 0.75 mile, the trail has a few switchbacks, a section of steps, and crosses Coal Creek on a footbridge before returning to the main trail.

Finish back at the start point. A nontechnical trail, save for a few exposed tree routes and rocks, this is a popular spot for families on day hikes, which can make for crowded weekend foot traffic.

BUYING NEW TRAIL-RUNNING SHOES

BEGIN BY LOOKING AT THE WEAR AND TEAR ON YOUR OLD, "SPENT" SHOES. Are the soles worn in certain parts and not in others? Wear patterns provide evidence of overpronation or supination. By looking at wet footprints left after a shower, bath, or swim and comparing your prints with others, you can determine relative arch height and forefoot width. Armed with those particular "foot notes," a trail runner is better able to shop for shoes at a local specialty running store, in a catalog, or from an online vendor, and better prepared to ask an expert salesperson for a recommendation. It is best to go to a running specialty store, where a foot specialist can perform a gait analysis using a videotaped treadmill or other test.

When shopping for trail shoes, wear the same kind of socks worn for running. Similarly, those who use

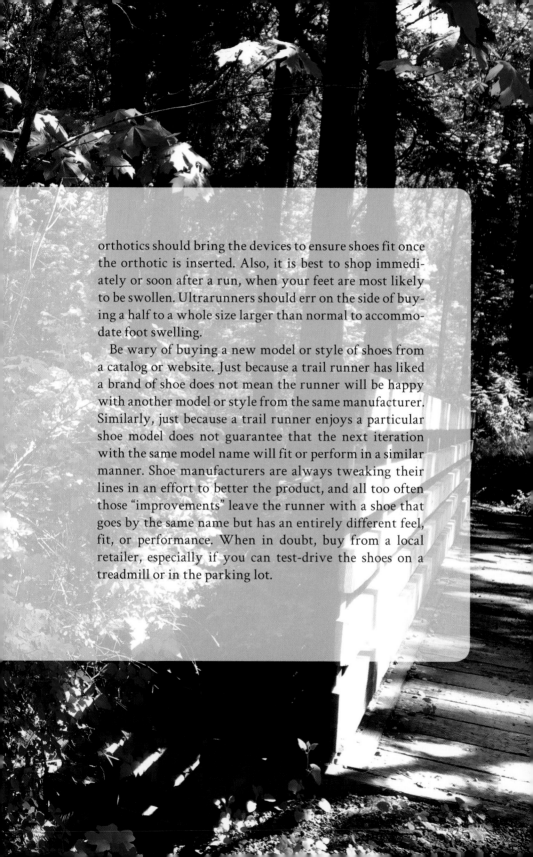

orthotics should bring the devices to ensure shoes fit once the orthotic is inserted. Also, it is best to shop immediately or soon after a run, when your feet are most likely to be swollen. Ultrarunners should err on the side of buying a half to a whole size larger than normal to accommodate foot swelling.

Be wary of buying a new model or style of shoes from a catalog or website. Just because a trail runner has liked a brand of shoe does not mean the runner will be happy with another model or style from the same manufacturer. Similarly, just because a trail runner enjoys a particular shoe model does not guarantee that the next iteration with the same model name will fit or perform in a similar manner. Shoe manufacturers are always tweaking their lines in an effort to better the product, and all too often those "improvements" leave the runner with a shoe that goes by the same name but has an entirely different feel, fit, or performance. When in doubt, buy from a local retailer, especially if you can test-drive the shoes on a treadmill or in the parking lot.

SQUAK MOUNTAIN STATE PARK/ COUGAR MOUNTAIN

THE COUGAR (28,000 ACRES), Squak Corridor (226 acres), Squak Mountain (1,545 acres), and Tiger Mountain (13,745 acres) parcels comprise more than 41,000 acres starting near Newcastle, south of I-405 and I-90, to WA 18. With numerous trail access points, there is limitless variety of terrain for trail runners of all abilities.

SQUAK/COUGAR MOUNTAIN CORRIDOR 6-MILE LOOP

THE RUN DOWN

START: Elevation 385 feet

OVERALL DISTANCE: 6-mile loop

APPROXIMATE RUNNING TIME: 90 minutes

DIFFICULTY: Blue

ELEVATION GAIN: 1,604 feet

BEST SEASON TO RUN: Year-round, but avoid in high winds or heavy rain

DOG FRIENDLY: Leashed dogs permitted

PARKING: Free

OTHER USERS: Equestrians; no cyclists

CELL PHONE COVERAGE: Fair to good

MORE INFORMATION: www .kingcounty.gov/services/ parks-recreation/parks/trails/ backcountry-trails/cougar-squak.aspx

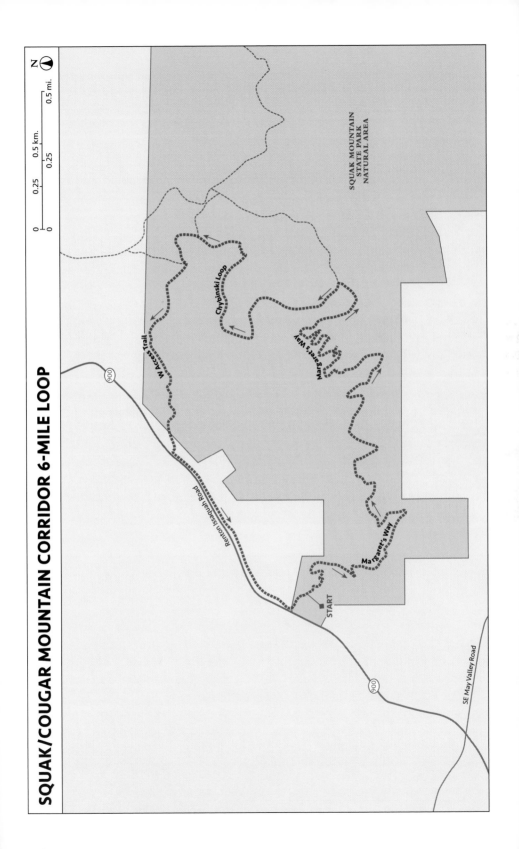

Squak Mountain - Squak/
Cougar Mountain Corridor
6-Mile Loop.
PHOTO BY NANCY HOBBS

FINDING THE TRAILHEAD

From Renton, head east on NE 4th Street, turn left on SE May Valley Road, then turn left on Renton-Issaquah Road NE/WA 900. Follow WA 900 approximately 0.75 mile to the parking lot on the right side of the street. The trailhead is just beyond the portable toilets by the kiosk and interpretive signage.

RUN DESCRIPTION

This is a very well-marked route starting on Margaret's Way, a trail that was dedicated in June 2015 in memory of long-time trail steward Margaret Macleod, who died from lung cancer. The trail starts as a wide, packed gravel-and-dirt path just uphill from the kiosk and after about 0.5 mile becomes mostly singletrack through lush forest, with the canopy overhead as well as some viewpoints along the way. With numerous switchbacks, the climbs don't seem quite as steep as it is. The surface includes exposed, and sometimes hidden, tree roots under a blanket of freshly fallen leaves.

In just under 3 miles, Margaret's Way reaches the intersection with Chybinski Loop Trail. Turn left on this mostly singletrack trail, which can

MAKE YOUR TRAIL SHOES LAST LONGER

The best way to prolong the life of trail shoes is to have several pairs and rotate them so that one pair is never used for more than a couple of consecutive runs without getting a rest. Using old beater pairs on days when the weather is particularly "sucky" also extends the life of newer shoes that you would rather not expose to brutal conditions. Like allowing the body to have recovery days, giving shoes some time off allows the midsole materials—the parts that usually break down the fastest—to decompress between runs.

It is a good idea to wash shoes by wiping them down to remove caked mud. Remove the insole inserts from the footbeds and insert balled-up newspaper in each footbed while the shoes dry at room temperature. If the shoes are soaked, it may be necessary to replace the newspaper once or twice.

It is best to allow shoes to dry slowly. That way they will be less likely to delaminate. Do not run the shoes through the washing machine or dryer or put them in the oven, as this can damage the midsole material. Reserve your favorite trail shoes for the activity they were made for: Do not wear them to work, for walking, or for hiking because that compresses and stresses them in ways that are not conducive to running—plus, such activities break them down prematurely.

Squak Mountain - Squak/Cougar Mountain Corridor 6-Mile Loop.
PHOTO BY NANCY HOBBS

have some puddles on rainy days. Be sure to run through puddles and not around them so as not to create social trails.

After about 1 mile, reach the West Access Trail and again turn left. Follow the trail over two footbridges and through one small creek crossing, heading mostly downhill. Reach WA 900 in about 0.75 mile. You can turn around for a 10-mile round-trip or turn left on WA 900 and run on the shoulder back to the start point, which is less than 1 mile. Be aware that trail crews continue to work on Margaret's Way, so there may be some improvements as well as rerouting in the coming years.

WILDERNESS CREEK TRAIL OUT-AND-BACK

THE RUN DOWN

START: Jim Whittaker Wilderness Peak Trailhead; elevation 404 feet

OVERALL DISTANCE: 1 mile out and back

APPROXIMATELY RUNNING TIME: 15 minutes

DIFFICULTY: Blue

ELEVATION GAIN: 441 feet

BEST SEASON TO RUN: Year-round

DOG FRIENDLY: Leashed dogs permitted

PARKING: Free

OTHER USERS: No bikes or horseback.

MORE INFORMATION: ftp:// ftp.kingcounty.gov/gis/ Web/VMC/recreation/BCT_ CougarMtn_brochure.pdf

FINDING THE TRAILHEAD

From Seattle, take I-90 E to WA 900 W. Look for the small parking lot on the north side of Renton-Issaquah Road SE (also known as WA 900), about 0.3 mile east of the parking lot for the Squak/Cougar Mountain Corridor (and just west of mile marker 19). The entrance to the parking lot is marked with a large blue sign (Cougar Mountain Regional Wildland Park/Jim Whittaker Wilderness Peak Trailhead), and there is a portable restroom in the parking lot. The trailhead is marked as the Whittaker Wilderness Creek Trail.

RUN DESCRIPTION

This route is at the southernmost end of Cougar Mountain Regional Wildland Park and can be the start point for many different trail connections of varying length.

Follow the trail through deep forest, across a small footbridge, and then up on singletrack with switchbacks sporting numerous exposed tree roots. After the second footbridge, located about 0.5 mile up the trail, there is a junction to connect with more trails. This is a turnaround for this short out-and-back.

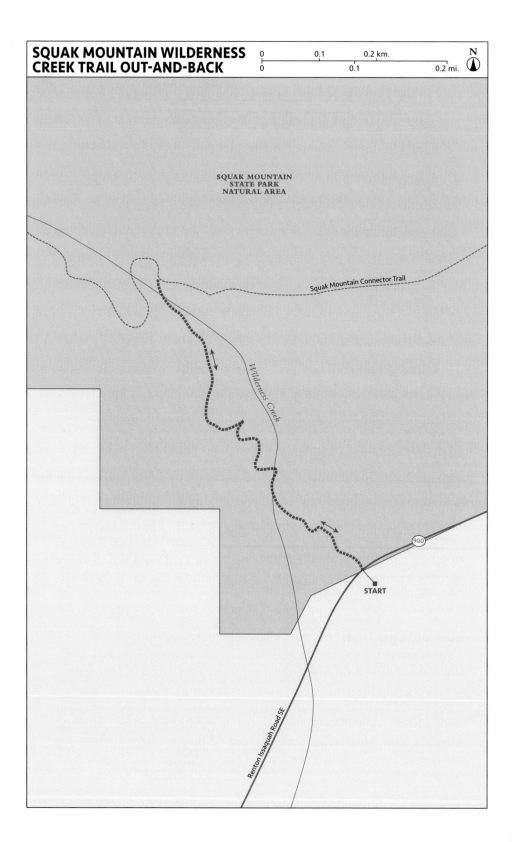

SQUAK MOUNTAIN WILDERNESS CREEK TRAIL OUT-AND-BACK

SQUAK MOUNTAIN
STATE PARK
NATURAL AREA

Squak Mountain Connector Trail

Wilderness Creek

900

START

Renton Issaquah Road SE

Squak Mountain - Wilderness Trail.
PHOTO BY NANCY HOBBS

But there are options. To the right, the Squak Mountain Corridor Trail connects back to WA 900, crossing over to the West Access Trail for more mileage into the Squak/Cougar Mountain Corridor. To the left, continue up the Wilderness Creek Trail and make a large lollipop loop back to the junction, or continue to explore the upper reaches of the park.

CENTRAL PEAK OUT-AND-BACK

THE RUN DOWN

START: SE May Valley Rd. entrance trailhead; elevation 367 feet

OVERALL DISTANCE: 6.1 miles out and back

APPROXIMATE RUNNING TIME: 95 minutes

DIFFICULTY: Blue

ELEVATION GAIN: 1,862 feet

BEST SEASON TO RUN: Year-round

DOG FRIENDLY: Leashed pets permitted

PARKING: A day-use fee is charged; an annual Discover Pass is also available, which is good at all Washington state parks

OTHER USERS: Equestrians, no cyclists

MORE INFORMATION: http://parks.state.wa.us/588/Squak-Mountain

FINDING THE TRAILHEAD

From Seattle, I-90 E to 405 S toward Renton at exit 10A. Follow Coal Creek Parkway SE to SE May Valley Road and use the SE May Valley Road entrance to the park, which is about halfway between WA 900 on the north and Issaquah-Hobart Road SE on the south. The parking lot has ample spaces for cars, as well as restroom facilities and an interpretive kiosk. The trailhead is directly across from the kiosk and restrooms.

SHOES FOR WOMEN

In the gender arena, many women are tired of purchasing shoes that were designed primarily for men, that were given the "shrink and pink" treatment for "the other sex" that is merely an afterthought. Fortunately, most manufacturers have acknowledged this deficiency and are now catering to female trail runners with specially engineered women's shoes. A handful of women's trail shoes on the market are manufactured on a woman's last, so check before purchasing if that affects fit and comfort.

SQUAK MOUNTAIN CENTRAL
PEAK OUT-AND-BACK

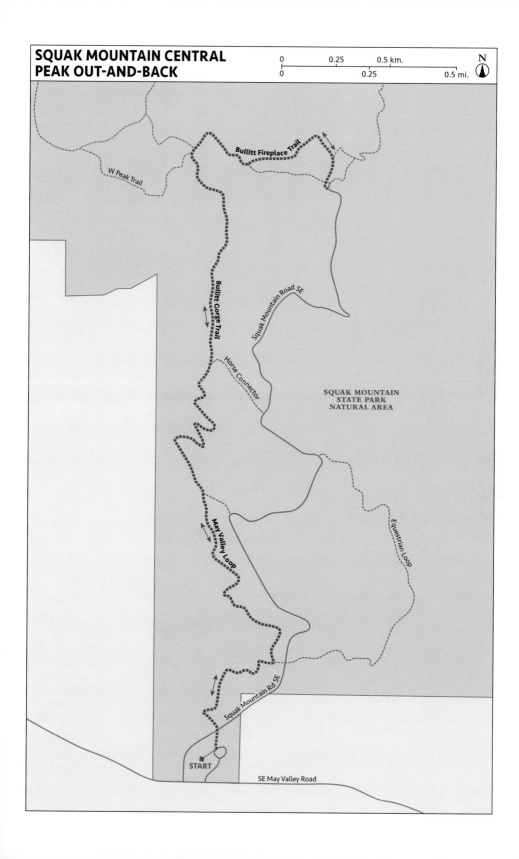

Squak Mountain - Central
Peak Out-and-Back.
PHOTO BY NANCY HOBBS

RUN DESCRIPTION

There are 13 miles of trails in Squak Mountain State Park, some of which connect to the Squak/Cougar Mountain Corridor. The trails are well signed and very well maintained.

For this out-and-back route, start on the May Valley Loop Trail and follow the signs to Central Peak. After less than 0.25 mile, cross a gravel road to the trail connector on the other side. From here, the route is almost entirely in the forest, with occasional breaks of sky light filtering through the trees overhead. The route includes several footbridges and two small creek crossings on mostly singletrack trail. Although there are switchbacks on the lower portions of the trail, after about 1.6 miles, the trail really narrows and the climb is technical and very steep, with tree roots and rocks hiding under the leaves.

The high point, at approximately 2,000 feet, is reached after 3 miles. This is the turnaround point. The summit is indicated by electric towers in a fenced enclosure. Retrace the route back to the parking lot, keeping in mind there are a few short uphill sections on the return trip.

For extra mileage, be sure to take a map and choose routes to the north, which connect to the Cougar/Squak Corridor and beyond.

TAYLOR MOUNTAIN

LOCATED SOUTH AND EAST OF TIGER MOUNTAIN, south of I-90 and east of WA 18 and between the communities of Hobart and North Bend, this area boasts 1,924 acres with thirty-three trails, including 10 miles of singletrack or doubletrack and 10 miles of forest service roads. With a variety of terrain, one of the trails offers sweeping views of Mount Rainier on a clear day. There are forested wetlands and meadows of wildflowers.

Taylor Mountain.
PHOTO BY NANCY HOBBS

TAYLOR MOUNTAIN

THE RUN DOWN

START: Trailhead on the east side of 276th Ave. SE; elevation 542 feet

OVERALL DISTANCE: 5.7-mile loop

APPROXIMATE RUNNING TIME: 65 minutes

DIFFICULTY: Green

ELEVATION GAIN: 977 feet

BEST SEASON TO RUN: Late spring, summer, and early fall; the Holder Creek Trail is closed October to April, primarily due to high water levels

DOG FRIENDLY: Leashed pets permitted on trails

PARKING: Free

OTHER USERS: Equestrians and mountain bikers

CELL PHONE COVERAGE: Very good

MORE INFORMATION: www .kingcounty.gov/services/ parks-recreation/parks/trails/ backcountry-trails/taylor-mtn.aspx

FINDING THE TRAILHEAD

Head east from Seattle on I-90 to Issaquah. Turn south onto Issaquah-Hobart Road SE, which passes under WA 18 and becomes 276th Avenue SE. The entrance to the parking lot, which was dedicated in May 2016, is 0.25 mile past WA 18 on the east side of 276th Avenue SE. There is a portable toilet in the parking area. The trailhead signage is very good, and there is ample parking for both cars and horse trailers. The trailhead is just north of the parking lot.

RUN DESCRIPTION

Start on the singletrack Holder Creek Trail for this clockwise route, and head left soon after crossing a maintained footbridge. The route is well marked (for the most part, although there are a few unmarked junctions, one of which travels about 0.5 mile to an open meadow with no connecting trails, requiring you to retrace your steps to the main trail).

Continue on mostly singletrack trail to the creek crossing of Holder Creek, which you have to cross twice, and there may be muddy spots on

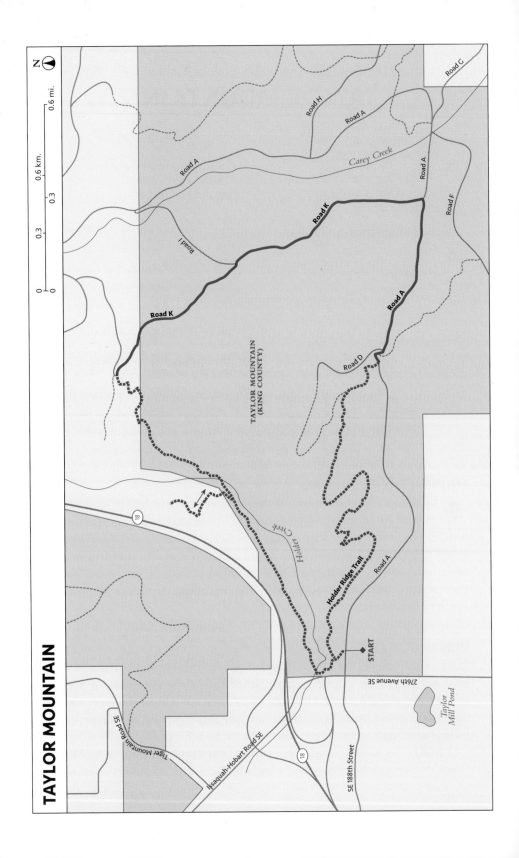

TAYLOR MOUNTAIN

Road G

Road H

Road A

Carey Creek

Road A

Road A

Road F

Road K

Road I

Road K

Road A

Road D

TAYLOR MOUNTAIN
(KING COUNTY)

Holder Creek

Holder Ridge Trail

Road A

START

276th Avenue SE

Taylor
Mill Pond

18

Tiger Mountain Road SE

Issaquah-Hobart Road SE

18

SE 188th Street

N

0.6 mi.

0.6 km.

0.3

0.3

0

0

Taylor Mountain.
PHOTO BY NANCY HOBBS

the trail near the creek. Some of the climbing, encountered after crossing the creek, has grades over 20 percent, as the trail rolls to where it connects with a wider fire road.

Turn right onto Road K, and there you'll find gently rolling terrain and some downhill sections until you connect to Road A. From Road A, take another right to get back on singletrack on the Holder Ridge Trail, which is yet another right turn. The Holder Ridge Trail returns to the start at the parking lot. For a short loop off Holder Trail, near the start of the trail off Road A, run the Holder Knob Loop for views of Mount Rainier on a clear day. In spring you may be treated to an abundance of strawberries and wild raspberries.

SPRING LAKE/ LAKE DESIRE PARK

THIS AREA IS A LIGHTLY TRAFFICKED GEM and embodies the tagline of King County Parks: "Your Big Backyard." Surrounded by neighborhoods, 390 acres encompass two lakes in this forested area, with 3 miles of mostly singletrack trails. Include some paved connections and you can extend your workout. Several adjoining parks, including Petrovitsky Park and McGarvey Park Open Space, offer additional trails on 1,000 acres and access points for parking. The area is also close to Lake Youngs Trail, a 10-mile route, which is 5 percent paved, 10 percent singletrack, and 85 percent dirt road, also featured in this guide.

Spring Lake. PHOTO BY NANCY HOBBS

3-MILE LOOP

FINDING THE TRAILHEAD

From Seattle, take I-5 S to the 405 N toward Renton. From the Maple Valley Highway, follow WA 169 (SE Petrovitsky Road). Take 196th Avenue SE, then SE 183rd Street, to East Spring Lake Drive SE. Follow that around the lake to the trailhead at the end of West Spring Lake Drive SE. There are limited parking spots.

RUN DESCRIPTION

Start on the gravel road just beyond the gate. Turn right and continue uphill on a second gravel roadway within the forest. After about 0.5 mile, turn right on a singletrack trail—signed Peak Trail—that is only open to foot traffic. Climb up wooden steps and enjoy twisting singletrack trails with more climbing, some of it at grades in excess of 29 percent and with rooted and rocky sections, to an overlook where, on a clear day, you'll

SPRING LAKE/LAKE DESIRE–
3-MILE LOOP

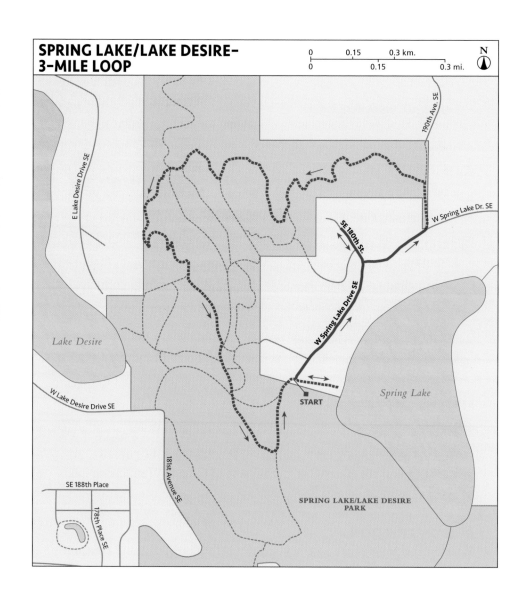

0   0.15   0.3 km.

0   0.15   0.3 mi.

N

190th Ave. SE

E Lake Desire Drive SE

W Spring Lake Dr. SE

SE 180th St.

W Spring Lake Drive SE

Lake Desire

Spring Lake

W Lake Desire Drive SE

START

181st Avenue SE

SE 188th Place

178th Place SE

SPRING LAKE/LAKE DESIRE
PARK

Spring Lake/Lake Desire - 3 Mile.
PHOTO BY NANCY HOBBS

enjoy a view of Mount Rainier from a small meadow at the summit of Cedar (Echo) Mountain.

Retrace your steps to another singletrack trail that winds through the forest and eventually dumps out on a gravel roadway that connects back to West Spring Lake Drive SE for a short run back to the parking lot near Spring Lake. It is wise to carry a map as there are unmarked sections of singletrack trail.

2.4-MILE OUT-AND-BACK

THE RUN DOWN

START: Trailhead at the end of W Spring Lake Dr. SE; elevation 509 feet

OVERALL DISTANCE: 2.4 miles out and back

APPROXIMATE RUNNING TIME: 25 minutes

DIFFICULTY: Green

ELEVATION GAIN: 55 feet

BEST SEASON TO RUN: Year-round; as this is a wetland area, the route can be muddy and slick in spots

DOG FRIENDLY: Leashed dogs permitted on trails

PARKING: Free

OTHER USERS: Equestrians, mountain bikers

CELL PHONE COVERAGE: Very good

MORE INFORMATION: ftp:// ftp.kingcounty.gov/gis/ Web/VMC/recreation/BCT_ SpringLkMcGarvey_brochure .pdf

Spring Lake/Lake Desire - 2.4 Mile.
PHOTO BY NANCY HOBBS

SPRING LAKE/LAKE DESIRE–
2.4-MILE OUT-AND-BACK

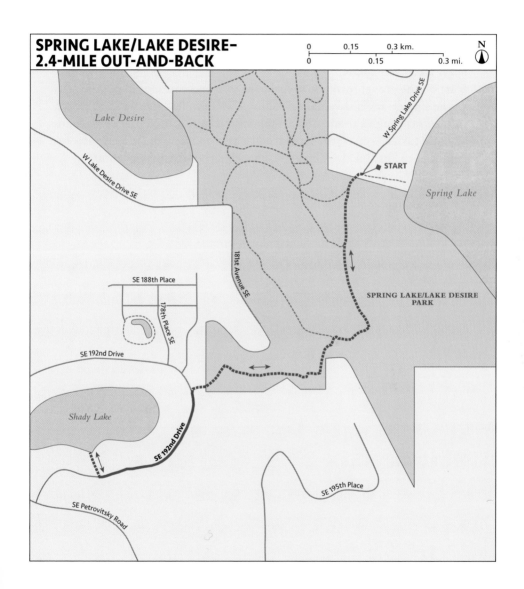

0   0.15   0.3 km.

0   0.15   0.3 mi.

N

Lake Desire

W Lake Desire Drive SE

W Spring Lake Drive SE

START

Spring Lake

SE 188th Place

778th Place SE

181st Avenue SE

SPRING LAKE/LAKE DESIRE
PARK

SE 192nd Drive

Shady Lake

SE 192nd Drive

SE 195th Place

SE Petrovitsky Road

FINDING THE TRAILHEAD

From the Maple Valley Highway, follow SR 169 (SE Petrovitsky Road). Take 196th Avenue SE, then SE 183rd Street to E Spring Lake Drive. Follow this road around the lake to the trailhead at the end of W Spring Lake Drive SE.

RUN DESCRIPTION

Start on the gravel road just beyond the gate and continue along the path to the singletrack Shady Lake Trail on the right. Follow the trail, which connects through a residential neighborhood just beyond the park boundary, and turn left on 179th Place SE and a loop on SE 196th Drive for an out-and-back to Shady Lake. Return on the same trail to the start point.

MCGARVEY PARK OPEN SPACE 8-MILE

IN THE KING COUNTY PARK SYSTEM, this open space area is comprised of 400 acres and over 5 miles of trails that connect with trails in the adjacent Spring Lake/Lake Desire Park.

McGarvey Park Open Space.
PHOTO BY NANCY HOBBS

MCGARVEY PARK OPEN SPACE 8-MILE

THE RUN DOWN

START: Stairs leading up from W Lake Desire Dr. SE; elevation 541 feet

OVERALL DISTANCE: 8 miles tour of the park

APPROXIMATE RUNNING TIME: 100 minutes

DIFFICULTY: Blue

ELEVATION GAIN: 1,274 feet

BEST SEASON TO RUN: Year-round, though as it is in wetlands, this route is often boggy and slick

DOG FRIENDLY: Leashed dogs permitted on trails

PARKING: Free

OTHER USERS: Equestrians and mountain bikers on designated trails

CELL PHONE COVERAGE: Good

MORE INFORMATION: www .kingcounty.gov/services/ parks-recreation/parks/parks-and-natural-lands/natural-lands/forest-stewardship/ mcgarvey.aspx

FINDING THE TRAILHEAD

Follow SE Petrovitsky Road north to SE 184th Street. Turn right and follow SE 184th Street to take a left on 172nd Avenue SE and a right on W Lake Desire Drive SE. Turn right at the junction with Woodside Drive SE and look for off-street parking along the wide gravel shoulder. The address for geo-locating devices is 17341 W Lake Desire Drive SE). The trail starts on the left side of W Lake Desire Drive SE and is indicated by steps leading uphill.

RUN DESCRIPTION

The trails in the area are relatively new, and, as of publication, there was no signage except for a sign that points the way to the Peak Trail, which is designated for foot traffic only. Be prepared to carry a map, a working cell phone, and, if you don't have them, bring along someone with navigation skills. It is very easy to get turned around on these trails, but the experience

MCGARVEY PARK OPEN SPACE 8-MILE

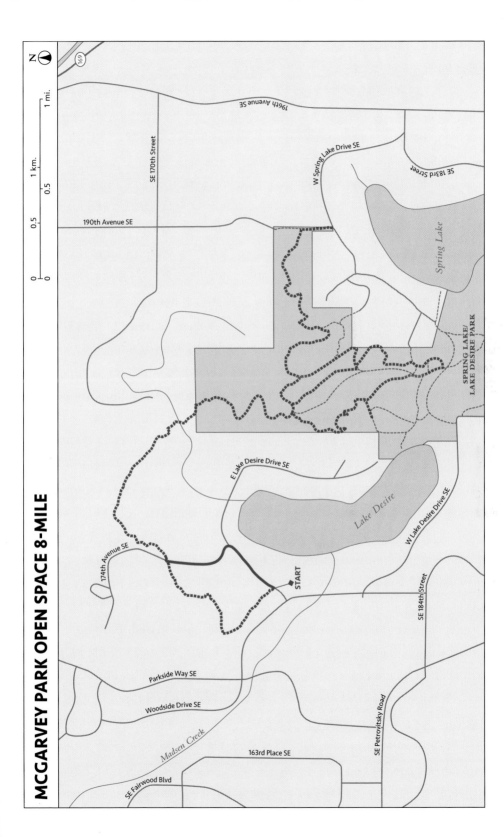

N

169

1 mi.

1 km.

0   0.5   0.5   1

196th Avenue SE

SE 170th Street

W Spring Lake Drive SE

SE 183rd Street

190th Avenue SE

Spring Lake

SPRING LAKE/
LAKE DESIRE PARK

E Lake Desire Drive SE

Lake Desire

W Lake Desire Drive SE

174th Avenue SE

START

SE 184th Street

Parkside Way SE

Woodside Drive SE

SE Petrovitsky Road

Madsen Creek

163rd Place SE

SE Fairwood Blvd

McGarvey Park Open Space.
PHOTO BY NANCY HOBBS

is fantastic as this urban setting delights and makes you feel the peaceful and serene nature of the wilderness within the forest.

Although this particular route encompasses many of the trails within McGarvey Open Space and Spring Lake/Lake Desire Park, an out-and-back 4-miler to the top of the Peak Trail, which reaches the summit of Cedar Mountain, is a pleasurable and much shorter endeavor.

On this route, the singletrack trails weave through the forest, with flat sections as well as rolling ascents and descents. Switchbacks, tight twists and turns, exposed tree roots, leaf-strewn paths, footbridges, climbing and descending . . . these trails have it all. The trails are underutilized, which provides a serene and secluded feel. On the upper reaches of the trail, near the approach to Cedar (Echo) Mountain, there are views of Lake Desire. On a clear day, you can see Mount Rainier from the summit.

EAST OF SEATTLE

Packs, Hydration Systems, Gel Flasks, and Water Filters

GIVEN THE PAUCITY OF WATER FOUNTAINS, SPIGOTS, or other conveniences on the typical trail run, most trail runners who run long enough to build up a thirst or hunger carry liquid and nutritional reserves. Depending on the temperature, projected length of run, availability of potable water, and the particular hydration and nutritional needs of an individual trail runner, it may be necessary to carry substantial quantities of drink and food on an excursion.

For shorter outings, a trail runner is likely to be able to get by without any liquids or food. But as temperatures rise and the distance of a run lengthens, trail runners will, at a minimum, need to carry a 16- or 20-ounce bottle or flask of water or electrolyte-replacement sports drink. Depending on preference, bottles may be carried in hand, either by simply gripping the bottle or with the assistance of a strap that fastens the bottle around the back of the hand, or in a lumbar or "fanny" pack. Modern lumbar packs are designed to distribute weight evenly throughout the lumbar region and often feature straight or angled pouches for bottles and separate pockets for food, clothing, and accessories. Some lumbar packs also include "gel holsters" for runners who carry a gel flask. Gel flasks hold up to five packs of sports gel for easy consumption and offer relief from sticky fingers or the need to pack out trash.

For longer runs, especially on trails that do not come in contact with sources of potable water, a hydration pack or multibottle carrier is probably necessary. Hydration packs have become common accessories in the evolving world of endurance sports because of their convenience and functionality. They incorporate a bladder or reservoir, delivery tube or hose, and a bite valve that allows trail runners to carry substantial quantities of fluid that is evenly distributed and consumed with hands-free ease. Other systems use a number of soft flasks that shrink when their contents are consumed. These packs are built more as form-fitting vests, with the flasks carried on the chest for easy access.

Hydration packs range in size and carrying capacity and come as backpacks, lumbar packs, and sports vests. Many hydration packs offer additional volume and storage pouches for food, clothing, and other trail necessities or conveniences. Certain bite valves are easier to use than others and some bladders are difficult to clean or keep free of bacteria, mold, mildew, and fungus. Others come with antimicrobial compounds, and some feature in-line water filters.

When running on trails that cross water sources, whether streams, creeks, rivers, ponds, lakes, or merely large puddles, trail runners can free themselves of substantial weight by carrying water filters and a single water bottle. Make sure the filter removes such evils as cryptosporidium, giardia, *E. coli*, volatile organic compounds, and other threatening substances common to the area where it is likely to be used. Note, however, that water filters do not protect against viruses. It may be necessary to use a combination of iodine tablets with a filter to assure the water is safe for consumption. Other devices use a charge to purify the water; another alternative is to use a filtered straw that allows you to pull filtered water directly from the source.

TOLT MACDONALD PARK

MOST NOTED FOR ITS CAMPING AND PICNICKING OPPORTUNITIES, this 574-acre park in the town of Carnation is one of the many parks in the King County Parks system. It sits at the confluence of the Tolt and Snoqualmie Rivers. Although some of the 12 miles of trails are of a more "primitive nature," they beg to be explored by the more adventurous trail runner. The park has a unique feature: a 500-foot-long suspension footbridge across the Snoqualmie River that connects the east and west sides of the park and offers views of the Cascade foothills. Just east of the park is the 31-mile packed-gravel multiuse Snoqualmie Valley Trail (http://northbendwa .gov/facilities.aspx?Page=detail&RID=8), running from Rattlesnake Lake in the south to Duvall in the north.

Tolt Mac Donald Park.
PHOTO BY NANCY HOBBS

TOLT MACDONALD PARK

THE RUN DOWN

START: From the parking lot near the Snoqualmie River suspension bridge; elevation 67 feet

OVERALL DISTANCE: 2.7-mile loop with an out-and-back on the north end

APPROXIMATE RUNNING TIME: 40 minutes

DIFFICULTY: Green, but the backcountry trails are challenging with elevation gain

ELEVATION GAIN: 449 feet

BEST SEASON TO RUN: Year-round, but be careful for mud and slick sections

DOG FRIENDLY: Leashed dogs permitted on trails

PARKING: Free

OTHER USERS: Equestrians and mountain bikers

CELL PHONE COVERAGE: Very good

MORE INFORMATION: www .kingcounty.gov/services/ parks-recreation/parks/parks- and-natural-lands/popular- parks/toltmacdonald.aspx

Tolt Mac Donald Park.
PHOTO BY NANCY HOBBS

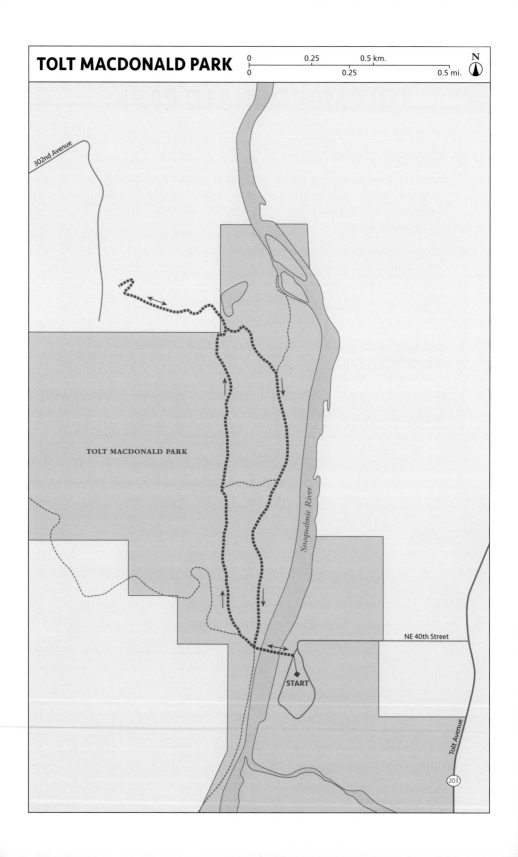

TOLT MACDONALD PARK

0   0.25   0.5 km.

0   0.25   0.5 mi.

N

302nd Avenue

TOLT MACDONALD PARK

Snoqualmie River

NE 40th Street

START

Tolt Avenue

203

FINDING THE TRAILHEAD

From Seattle, take I-5 N to WA 520 E to WA 202 E to NE Tolt Road to NE 40th Street. (Another route to the north of the park . . . take WA 203 to Carnation and head west on NE 40th Street.) From near the parking lot, start your run on NE 40th Street, and cross over the Snoqualmie River on a 500-foot suspension bridge. Stop to enjoy the view of the river and the Cascade foothills, and then turn right onto a gravel pathway that leads to the trails.

RUN DESCRIPTION

Follow the signs for the Cottonwood Trail, and head in a clockwise direction. After 1 mile, turn left and explore some of the more primitive trails, which include some steep climbs, some overgrown foliage, and a steep descent on the initial out-and-back section. Return to the rolling single-track trails within the forest, and take the North Shelter Loop Trail back to the parking lot.

SOARING EAGLE REGIONAL PARK

THIS KING COUNTY PARK HAS 12 MILES OF TRAILS WITHIN ITS 600 ACRES. The trails are very well marked, but there are a lot of junctions so it is wise to carry a photocopy of the trail map to better navigate your intended route. Even during the week, there is quite a bit of activity in the park, with mountain bikers, dog walkers, hikers, and runners enjoying the trails. The trails are gently rolling, but it is necessary to watch your footing as there are sections with exposed roots and rocks. Many of the trails are singletrack, but the Pipeline Trail is a wider pathway of packed gravel.

SOARING EAGLE REGIONAL PARK

THE RUN DOWN

START: At the trailhead on the north end of the parking lot; elevation 488 feet

OVERALL DISTANCE: 2.2-mile loop

APPROXIMATE RUNNING TIME: 25 minutes

DIFFICULTY: Green

ELEVATION GAIN: 140 feet

BEST SEASON TO RUN: Year-round

DOG FRIENDLY: Leashed dogs permitted on trails

PARKING: Free; there are approximately fifteen spots

OTHER USERS: Equestrians and mountain bikers

CELL PHONE COVERAGE: Very good

MORE INFORMATION: www .kingcounty.gov/services/ parksrecreation/parks/trails/ backcountry-trails/soaring-eagle.aspx

SOARING EAGLE REGIONAL PARK

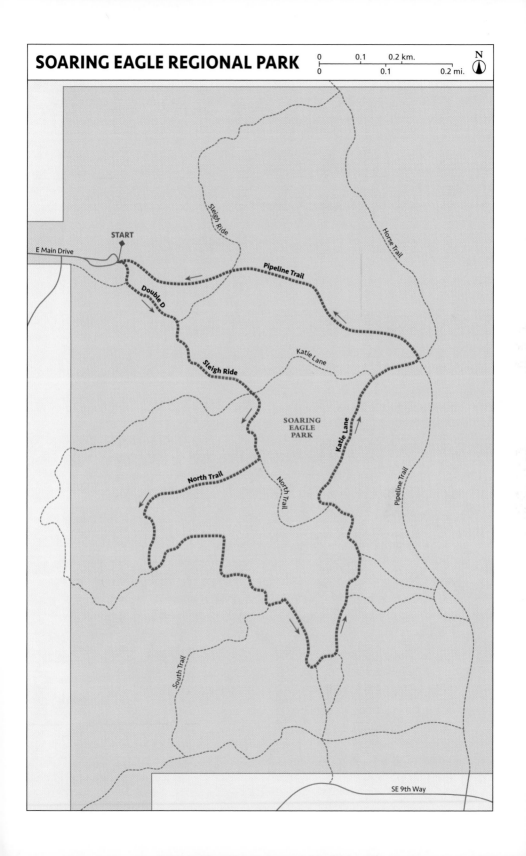

0   0.1   0.2 km.

0   0.1   0.2 mi.

N

Sleigh Ride

Horse Trail

START

E Main Drive

Pipeline Trail

Double D

Sleigh Ride

Katie Lane

SOARING
EAGLE
PARK

Katie Lane

North Trail

North Trail

Pipeline Trail

South Trail

SE 9th Way

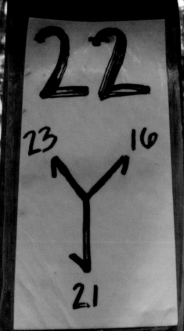

Soaring Eagle Regional Park.
PHOTO BY NANCY HOBBS

FINDING THE TRAILHEAD

From Seattle, take I-5 North to 520 E to 202 E. Turn right on 244th Avenue NE and then left on E Main Drive. The drive to the trailhead is on residential roads through attractive neighborhoods. The park is at 26015 E Main Drive in Sammamish. There is a portable toilet at the trailhead and parking for fifteen cars, as well as trailer parking for equestrians. The well-signed trailhead is located on the north side of the parking lot.

RUN DESCRIPTION

This is a very well-marked route, and a trail map features corresponding trail numbers indicated on posts at all junctions, of which there are many. This short, counterclockwise loop in the forest provides a good overview of the park, with rolling singletrack sections and a wider path at the finish. Keep your eyes open for the many rocks and exposed tree roots along the trail.

This route starts on the Double D Trail, which is a singletrack trail connecting to the Sleigh Ride Trail, the North Trail, and the Northwest Passage Trail complete with many twists and turns, switchbacks, exposed rocks and roots. The singletrack section connects with the wider gravel pathway—the Pipeline Trail—after about 1.6 miles leading back to the start point. Most of the route is forested, save the final few feet of the Pipeline Trail.

Soaring Eagle Regional Park.
PHOTO BY NANCY HOBBS

LAKE YOUNGS TRAIL

LOCATED NEAR RENTON, THIS TRAIL IS NOT OVERLY SCENIC, but provides an off-road opportunity in an urban setting. The complete loop is just under 10 miles and can be run in a clockwise or counterclockwise direction. The surface varies from wide, hard-packed gravel path to sections of singletrack dirt trail, much of which runs parallel to SE Petrovitsky Road. The trail is well marked in its entirety.

Lake Youngs Trail.
PHOTO BY NANCY HOBBS

LAKE YOUNGS TRAIL

THE RUN DOWN

START: At the trailhead on SE Old Petrovitsky Rd.; elevation 590 feet

OVERALL DISTANCE: 6 miles out and back

APPROXIMATE RUNNING TIME: 60 minutes

DIFFICULTY: Green

ELEVATION GAIN: 470 feet

BEST SEASON TO RUN: Year-round

DOG FRIENDLY: Leashed dogs permitted

PARKING: Free

OTHER USERS: Mountain bikers, equestrians

CELL PHONE COVERAGE: Very good

MORE INFORMATION: www .alltrails.com/trail/us/ washington/lake-youngs

Lake Youngs Trail.
PHOTO BY NANCY HOBBS

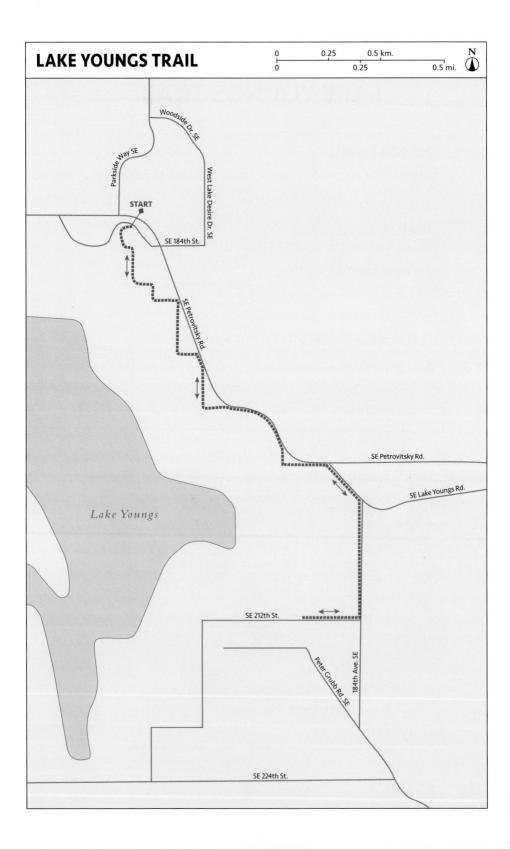

LAKE YOUNGS TRAIL

0   0.25   0.5 km.

0   0.25   0.5 mi.

N

Woodside Dr. SE

Parkside Way SE

West Lake Desire Dr. SE

START

SE 184th St.

SE Petrovitsky Rd.

SE Petrovitsky Rd.

SE Lake Youngs Rd.

Lake Youngs

SE 212th St.

Peter Grubb Rd. SE

184th Ave. SE

SE 224th St.

Lake Youngs Trail.
PHOTO BY NANCY HOBBS

FINDING THE TRAILHEAD

From Seattle, take I-5 S to 405 N. Continue to WA 169 S and turn right on 140th Way SE, then left on SE Petrovitsky Road. A parking lot with a toilet facility is located on SE Old Petrovitsky Road, south of SE Petrovitsky Road. The trailhead is located on the south side of the parking lot.

RUN DESCRIPTION

Follow the crushed gravel path approximately 200 yards to the start of the trail and turn left. Continue for 3 miles for this out-and-back mapped route, which includes sections of wider, crushed gravel as well as single-track, and dirt trail. Run alongside a chain link fence for the majority of the route, never too far from SE Petrovitsky Road or SE Lake Youngs Road.

SELECTING THE RIGHT SHOE

TO HELP TAKE THE MYSTERY OUT OF TRAIL SHOE PUR-CHASES, you can save time and effort by categorizing yourself as a certain "type" of trail runner. Consider which of the following characteristics best describe you as a trail runner: stable or unstable, heavy or light, nimble or clumsy, hot or cold, cheap or lavish, ultra, rugged, versatile, or fashionable? Keep in mind that a single shoe style may not apply to a single runner type. Indeed, trail runners may own multiple pairs of trail shoes and use them for different types of runs.

The following questions should help determine your type for purposes of selecting appropriate trail shoes:

- Are you injury prone?
- Do you need special support or stability built into the running shoes?
- Do you emphasize fashion or function?
- For what types of terrain will the shoes be used?
- How many miles are expected from the shoes before retirement?
- Is breathability or waterproofness of uppers important?
- How much can you spend?
- What distance runs will the shoes be worn for?
- Is it important that the shoe be designed for women?
- Are your feet sensitive to bone bruises?
- Do you have odd-size or oddly shaped feet?

- Is shoe weight an important factor?
- Are the shoe's cushioning, flexibility, heel-toe drop, and agility particularly important?

By answering these questions, you can make more informed purchasing decisions. You will also be better able to find a replacement for a favorite shoe style when the manufacturer discontinues or completely changes the model after only a season or two.

SHOE CONSTRUCTION

From the bottom up, a trail shoe usually has a more aggressive tread, or outsole, and deeper lugs than a road shoe. The outsole provides traction and is usually made of a durable carbon rubber and/or other compounds to enhance traction, stabilize or smooth out the "ride," control motion, and increase longevity.

The next level up, the "midsole," is the heart of a trail shoe. The midsole is usually made of ethylene vinyl acetate ("EVA") or polyurethane ("PU") to provide most of the cushioning, support, and stability. The decision to retire a trail shoe should depend on the compression of the midsole. Those shoes that feature relatively firm midsoles tend to provide a more rigid ride, but they also offer underfoot protection and allow runners to "feel" the trail.

A trail shoe's midsole composition also determines its profile, or how low to the ground the foot sits in the shoe. A low profile offers a greater sense of contact with or "feel" for the trail. Although a low profile enhances agility, it provides less protection from bone bruises. On the other hand, a more substantial midsole offers greater cushioning, but limits the ability to feel the trail, performing more like an RV than a sports car. Manufacturers may integrate multiple materials into the midsole to help give the shoe more stability for runners who supinate or overpronate. Some trail shoes also feature reinforcements, such as a fabric weave or a carbon plate, in the midsole to protect the foot from bone bruises. Shoe companies also integrate various gel capsules, air compartments, or other cushioning devices into midsoles. While some of these shock-absorbing devices work well for road shoes, they are often little more than gimmicks when it comes to trail shoes.

The next layer is the sock liner, which may be removed to accommodate orthotics, arch supports, or other corrective devices. Topping off the entire shoe is the upper, which secures the foot to the midsole. Uppers are usually constructed of mesh, leather, synthetic leather, or a waterproof breathable fabric in various combinations. Mesh is best for runs in warm, hot weather or wet weather, as water can easily escape. Waterproof uppers work well for runs in cooler climes, assuming no water or snow melt is around to seep in around the ankle collar. Waterproof shoes tend to heat up and retain any moisture or condensation that accumulates on the inside. Because of increased abrasion from the trail, trail shoe uppers often feature reinforcements, such as hefty toe bumpers. Trail shoe uppers usually provide more lateral support than road shoes. Much of this support and stability comes from the heel counter, which holds the foot in place over the footbed.

The lacing systems of trail shoes allow runners to choose from a variety of fastening options that adjust the fit for comfort, pressure distribution, and stability. Many trail shoes also feature more flexible laces that reduce pressure on the instep and tend to stay tied when wet.

SHOE TYPES

For runners who log most of their miles on pavement and only a small fraction on trails, a road shoe may be the best choice. Alternatively, runners who frequent a mix of paved roads and trails might consider hybrid shoes that, for all intents and purposes, are road shoes with a beefier outsole, toe bumper, and earthier colors.

Trail runners who spend most of their time on single-track, sand, scree, ice, mud, gravel, rock, and other challenging off-road surfaces should look for trail shoes with aggressive tread patterns. Keep in mind that softer outsole materials effectively grip rocky surfaces but wear more quickly than harder carbon rubber.

Another consideration is the number of miles you can reasonably expect from the shoes before they must be retired, coupled with how much you are willing to spend on the footwear purchase. A related concern is to anticipate the usual distance over which the shoes will be worn. Cross-country runners gravitate to lighter shoes with very aggressive outsoles and minimal support or cushioning. Trail ultramarathoners want shoes that give plenty of support, breathe well, and have midsoles that remain consistent over different types of surfaces and under different weather conditions. One thing high-altitude and ultrarunners should be aware of when purchasing shoes is the almost inevitable expansion of their feet at high elevation or after hours of running. Many experienced trail runners buy shoes at least a half-size larger than normal to accommodate this common occurrence.

Special Considerations

You should consider the likely weather conditions and your individual needs for ventilation, waterproofing, or warmth when selecting trail-running shoes. For example, a runner likely to be running in wet weather or through mud, slush, or puddles may want to consider a shoe that shields out water or is sufficiently breathable to enable

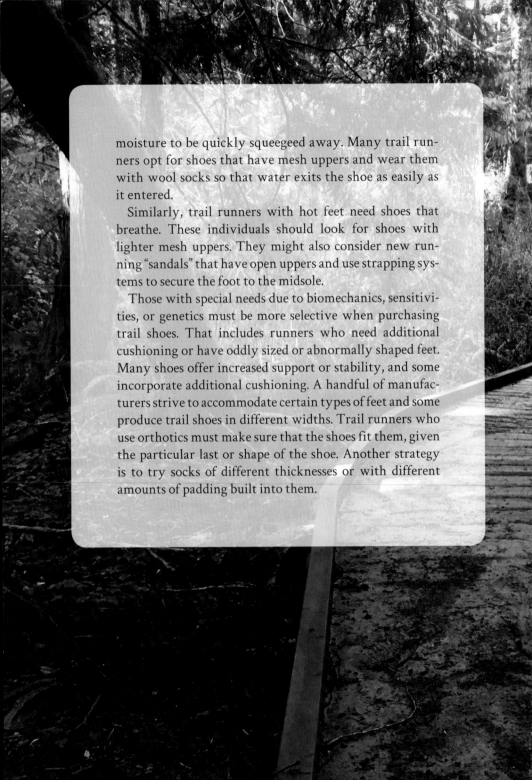

moisture to be quickly squeegeed away. Many trail runners opt for shoes that have mesh uppers and wear them with wool socks so that water exits the shoe as easily as it entered.

Similarly, trail runners with hot feet need shoes that breathe. These individuals should look for shoes with lighter mesh uppers. They might also consider new running "sandals" that have open uppers and use strapping systems to secure the foot to the midsole.

Those with special needs due to biomechanics, sensitivities, or genetics must be more selective when purchasing trail shoes. That includes runners who need additional cushioning or have oddly sized or abnormally shaped feet. Many shoes offer increased support or stability, and some incorporate additional cushioning. A handful of manufacturers strive to accommodate certain types of feet and some produce trail shoes in different widths. Trail runners who use orthotics must make sure that the shoes fit them, given the particular last or shape of the shoe. Another strategy is to try socks of different thicknesses or with different amounts of padding built into them.

WEST OF SEATTLE

BAINBRIDGE ISLAND

MAKE A DAY OF IT AND HEAD TO BAINBRIDGE ISLAND TO ENJOY THE TRAILS. Partake in a pastry from Blackbird Bakery or Bainbridge Bakers before your run, and enjoy sandwiches to go from the Town and Country Market (remodeled in 2016) for your trip on the ferry back to Seattle.

You can also stay for a stroll through the world-renowned gardens at Bloedel Reserve, followed by a craft brew at Bainbridge Island Brewery. For shopping enjoyment, the main street adjacent to the ferry terminal features boutique shops sporting fashionable items and the work of local artisans.

Bainbridge Island.
PHOTO BY NANCY HOBBS

GRAND FOREST WEST LOOP

THE RUN DOWN

START: The trailhead at 9752 Miller Rd. NE; elevation 150 feet

OVERALL DISTANCE: 2.8-mile loop

APPROXIMATE RUNNING TIME: 30 minutes

DIFFICULTY: Green

ELEVATION GAIN: 272 feet

BEST SEASON TO RUN: Year-round; the trails have good drainage, albeit a puddle or two may remain after a rain

DOG FRIENDLY: Leashed dogs permitted on the trails

PARKING: Free

OTHER USERS: Equestrians, mountain bikers

CELL PHONE COVERAGE: Good

MORE INFORMATION: www .biparks.org/biparks_site/ parks/grand-forest.htm

FINDING THE TRAILHEAD

Approximately 4.5 miles from the Ferry Terminal, turn right onto 305 N. Turn left onto Madison Avenue N, then immediate right onto NE New Brooklyn Road. Turn right onto Miller Road NE and the trailhead is located at 9752 Miller Road NE. There is a small lot (ten spots) at the trailhead. If the lot is full, some on-street parking may be available along the shoulder of the road.

RUN DESCRIPTION

What is so enjoyable about this area is the variety of options offered by the 8 miles of trails winding through 240 acres of lush firs, cedars, maples, and a few giant conifers. This loop is described in a clockwise direction, and although the trail is marked, it is a bit confusing for a first-timer, as intermittent distance markers are staked in the ground seemingly not relating to a specific trail. For this loop, choose the left fork at any intersection.

The route is wide singletrack from the start, with a short section on packed dirt/gravel on the Hilltop section in a glorious meadow that

BAINBRIDGE ISLAND–GRAND FOREST WEST LOOP

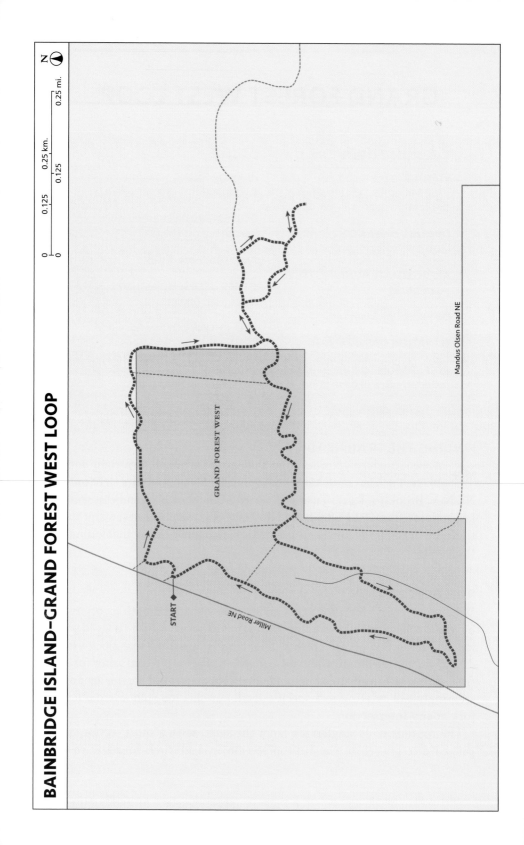

N

0   0.125   0.25 km.
0   0.125   0.25 mi.

GRAND FOREST WEST

Mandus Olsen Road NE

START

Miller Road NE

Bainbridge Island.
PHOTO BY NANCY HOBBS

provides—on a clear day—a view of the Olympic range. There is a trail connector on the east side of the Hilltop Trail to the Grand Forest East trails. Primarily passing through old-growth forest replete with trees sporting mossy growth from trunk to towering branches, the terrain is hard-packed—although rooted in spots—but affords good absorption during rainy months due to packed mulch underfoot. On the route, a wooden bridge spans a creek and a short section of boardwalk runs next to a small pond.

FOREST-TO-SKY LOOP

The Forest-to-Sky trailhead is across Miller Road and just west of the parking lot for the Grand Forest West loop run. This route is on wide single-track, similar to that found in the Grand Forest trail system, and leads, in just under 1 mile, to a packed gravel connection to the Battle Point Park Trail, which provides a 1.25-mile loop around two duck ponds on flat terrain. This route is unique because it has a section in the forest as well as a more open urban vibe through a park.

THE RUN DOWN

START: The trailhead across the street from 9752 Miller Rd. NE; elevation 161 feet

OVERALL DISTANCE: 3.1-mile loop

APPROXIMATE RUNNING TIME: 30 minutes

DIFFICULTY: Green

ELEVATION GAIN: 210 feet

BEST SEASON TO RUN: Year-round, due to the solid drainage. This being the Pacific Northwest, you will likely see post-rain puddles

DOG FRIENDLY: Leashed dogs permitted

PARKING: Free

OTHER USERS: Equestrians, mountain bikers

CELL PHONE COVERAGE: Good

MORE INFORMATION: www .biparks.org/biparks_site/ trails/trail-finder.htm#forest-to-sky

FINDING THE TRAILHEAD

 The trailhead is located at 9752 Miller Road NE, across the road from the Grand Forest West parking area.

BAINBRIDGE ISLAND–FOREST-TO-SKY LOOP

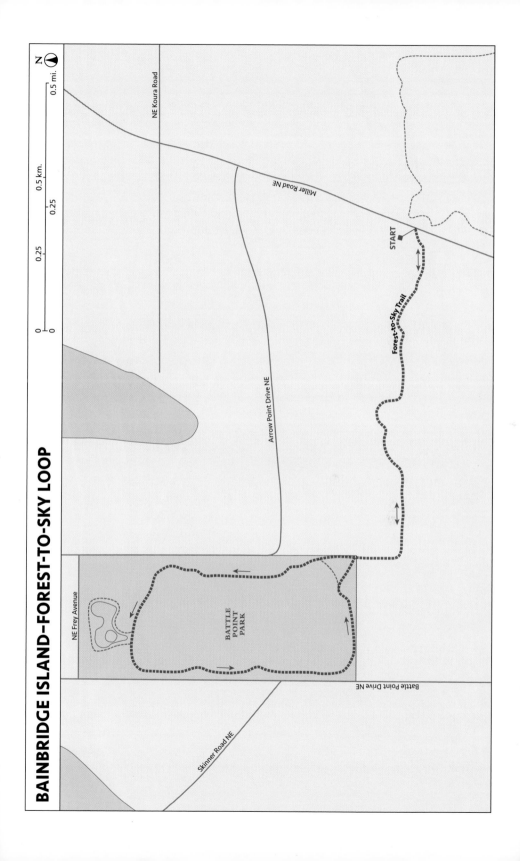

N

0.5 mi.

0   0.25   0.5 km.
0   0.25   0.5 mi.

NE Koura Road

Miller Road NE

START

Forest-to-Sky Trail

Arrow Point Drive NE

NE Frey Avenue

BATTLE
POINT
PARK

Battle Point Drive NE

Skinner Road NE

Bainbridge Island.

Bainbridge Island.
PHOTO BY NANCY HOBBS

RUN DESCRIPTION

Cross Miller Road just west of the parking lot for the Forest-to-Sky Trail-head. This section is on wide singletrack similar to that found in the Grand Forest trail system and leads, in just under 1 mile, to a packed gravel connection to the Battle Point Park Trail, which provides a 1.25-mile loop around two duck ponds on flat terrain. This route is unique because it has a section in the forest as well as a more open urban vibe through a park.

ReCOVeRY, ReST, and COMMON SeNSe

MORE IS NOT ALWAYS BETTER. This is sometimes the most difficult lesson for trail runners to fully absorb. Failure to learn the lesson leads to acute injury or chronic suboptimal performance. Even ultrarunners know that some rest, even if only active rest through cross-training, enhances their running performance. Just as the need exists to integrate recovery and rest into repeat or interval training to get the most from each repeat or interval, periods of recovery and rest should be integrated into your overall training schedule. It often takes more discipline to take a day off than to go hard or long.

With proper recovery and rest, trail runners are able to attack hard days and make them worthwhile. Without recovery and rest, the pace of hard runs and easy runs will be approximately the same, and very little benefit will result from either. If you are the type who is likely to overdo it, keep a running log or journal that tracks your daily runs, noting time, effort, mileage, and other pertinent factors such as weather, cross-training activities, sleep, diet, work load, emotional state, stress level, terrain, and if you know them, altitude, and heart rate. Those daily entries will force you to face the question of whether you are doing quality runs as opposed to sheer quantity. The diary will also give an indication of whether you are overtraining. When you notice progress in your running, you will be in a better position to recall and evaluate what factors worked to produce that success.

Another alternative for those who lack the discipline for proper recovery and rest is to get a coach. Although not many coaches specialize in trail training, a good running coach will be able to help develop a customized training schedule that takes into consideration a runner's personal strengths and weaknesses. A coach should also help integrate recovery days and rest into your training.

Only so much fuel is in any runner's tank, and if it isn't replenished between workouts, that reservoir will soon be running on empty. While it is a worthwhile training experience to overstress your system and run on "fumes," that should be a rare exception rather than the rule. Depriving the body of proper recovery and rest is like running without adequate food or drink; eventually breakdown will occur, at which point you'll have to stop for longer than if you had worked adequate recovery and rest periods into the training schedule.

To assure that easy days or recovery runs are not overly strenuous, arrange to run with someone who is willing to run at a moderate pace. Avoid running with someone who has a proclivity to pick it up or with whom you tend to be competitive. Consider running without a watch, or wear a heart rate monitor that can be set to warn if a predetermined rate is exceeded. Be open to the idea of walking ascents, stopping to stretch, or simply to smell the flowers and enjoy a vista.

A trail runner may boast of having put in a solid month of 120-mile weeks, yet show little to no benefit from such high mileage. Alternatively, a runner who puts in as little as 30 to 40 miles a week in three or four runs can show tremendous progress if each of those runs serves a particular training purpose. Design the easy days to accomplish a purpose, and transfer any pent-up energy to the hard or long days to really make those workouts count toward improvement.

Although trail running may not beat a runner up the way road or track running does, it is still important to incorporate recovery and rest into training. Recovery and rest periods should come between repeats and intervals, between hard workouts, and before and after races. The use of recovery and rest also applies on a macro level, such as in scheduling a particular season or year to build up to a specific running goal. A trail runner often picks a race as far off as a year, then trains with that race in mind, perhaps running several "training" races geared to preparing for "the target" race.

The training principle of "periodization" (also called "phase" training) is based on the idea that an athlete may reach a performance peak by building up through a set of steps, each of which may last for weeks or months, depending on the starting point and where the athlete wants to be at the peak of the periodization training. Periodization training starts with a build-up or foundation period, upon which a base of endurance and strength is built. From there, the athlete works on speed and endurance, incorporating distance, tempo runs, intervals, repeats, and fartleks. Once the fitness and strength levels are sufficient to run the target distance at a pace that is close to the goal, focus is reoriented to speed work and turnover to tweak muscles for a fast pace. It is at this point that the athlete is ready for a recovery phase, also known as the "taper" period.

Within the big picture of a periodization schedule, you should be prepared to make micro adjustments for recovery and rest to stave off overtraining or injury. Know your body and be aware of heightened heart rate; sleep problems; loss of appetite; a short temper; a general lack of enthusiasm; tight or sore muscles, bones, and connective tissue; or other symptoms of burnout. Get adequate sleep with a consistent sleep routine. Quality of rest is probably more important than quantity, and playing catch-up does not always work to restore your body to a rested state. Also be sure to eat a balanced diet with adequate calories and fluids to power through the workout and the entire day.

Engaging in yoga or meditation can play a useful part in the recovery and rest phase. Just because you are not running trails during your time off doesn't mean you must sacrifice the peace of mind gained from running in a beautiful place. Those who practice meditative arts are able to reach a similar state of equanimity and tranquility as that gained by running trails, without lifting a foot. Another restorative measure, if available, is a sauna, hot tub, or steam room. The benefits of sports massage are also likely to be worth the time and cost.

When determining the amount of recovery and rest needed, consider the impact of other life events and the effect that family, work, travel, social, and emotional lives have on training—and vice versa. The need may arise to run more or less during particularly stressful periods, regardless of the specific point in the periodization schedule. If emotionally drained, a long slow run in a scenic environment might replace what was supposed to be a hard hill repeat day.

Know yourself, set reasonable short- and long-term goals, and be willing to adjust them. Be flexible and avoid imposing on yourself a training partner's or someone else's goals. Every trail runner is an individual and responds to different types of training. What works for one trail runner might be a huge mistake for another. Be sensitive to all of your needs, plus those of family, friends, and coworkers.

A holistic approach to trail running will keep training in perspective. Yes, you need to respect the importance of adequate training, but do not miss the forest for the trees. You will be better able to run the trail that leads through those

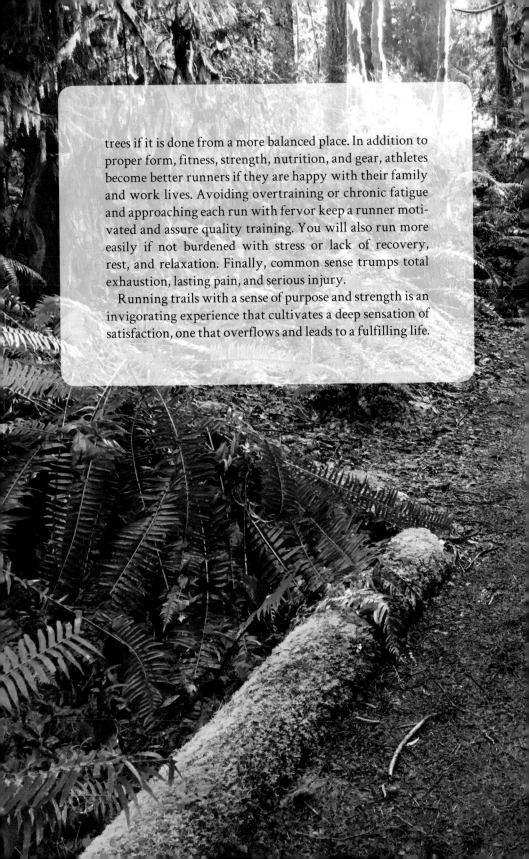

trees if it is done from a more balanced place. In addition to proper form, fitness, strength, nutrition, and gear, athletes become better runners if they are happy with their family and work lives. Avoiding overtraining or chronic fatigue and approaching each run with fervor keep a runner motivated and assure quality training. You will also run more easily if not burdened with stress or lack of recovery, rest, and relaxation. Finally, common sense trumps total exhaustion, lasting pain, and serious injury.

Running trails with a sense of purpose and strength is an invigorating experience that cultivates a deep sensation of satisfaction, one that overflows and leads to a fulfilling life.

APPENDIX A: ATRA RULES ON THE RUN

"Rules on the Run" are principles of trail-running etiquette that foster environmentally sound and socially responsible trail running. These principles emulate the well-established principles of Leave No Trace (https://lnt.org) and Rules of the Trail (https://www.imba.com/about/rules-trail) by the International Mountain Biking Association (IMBA). The American Trail Running Association (ATRA; www.trailrunner.com) believes that by educating trail runners to observe Rules on the Run, they will be able to enjoy continued access to their favorite trails and trail-running competitions.

1. **Stay on the Trail:** Well-marked trails already exist; they are not made on the day you head out for a run (i.e., making your own off-trail path). There is nothing cool about running off trail, bushwhacking over and under trees, or cutting switchbacks up the side of a hill or mountain. Such running creates new trails, encourages others to follow in your footsteps (creating unmarked "social trails"), and increases the runner's footprint on the environment. When multiple trails exist, run on the one that is the most worn. Stay off closed trails and obey all posted regulations.

2. **Run over Obstacles:** Run single file in the middle of a trail, even when muddy or laden with a fresh blanket of snow. Go through puddles and not around them. Running around mud, rocks, or downed tree limbs widens trails, impacts vegetation, and causes further and unnecessary erosion. Use caution when going over obstacles, but challenge yourself by staying in the middle of the trail. If the terrain is exceedingly muddy, refrain from running on the trails so that you don't create damaging "potholes" in the surface. Moisture is the chief factor that determines how traffic (from any user group) affects a trail. For some soil types, a 100-pound runner can wreak havoc on a trail surface in extremely wet conditions. In dry conditions, the same trail might easily withstand a 1,200-pound horse/rider combination. There are many situational factors to consider when making your trail-running decision. Trails that have been constructed with rock work or those with soils that drain quickly may hold up to wet conditions—even a downpour. But, in general, if the trail is wet enough to become muddy and hold puddles, *all* user groups should avoid it until the moisture has drained.

3. **Run Only on Officially Designated Open Trails:** Respect trail and road closures and avoid trespassing on private land. Get permission

first to enter and run on private land. Obtain permits or authorizations that may be required for some wilderness areas and managed trail systems. Leave gates as you've found them. If you open a gate, be sure to close it behind you. Make sure the trails you run on are officially designated routes, not user-created routes. When in doubt, ask the land managing agency or individuals responsible for the area you are using.

4. **Respect Animals:** Do not disturb or harass wildlife or livestock. Animals scared by your sudden approach may be dangerous. Give them plenty of room to adjust to you. Avoid trails that cross known wildlife havens during sensitive times such as nesting or mating. When passing horses, use special care and follow directions from the horseback riders. Running cattle is a serious offense. Consider turning around and going another direction when faced with disturbing large herds of animals, especially in winter when animals are highly stressed already.

5. **Keep Your Dog on a Leash:** Unless otherwise posted, keep your dog on a leash and under control at all times. Dogs running off-leash may result in adverse impacts on terrain and wildlife and degrade the outdoor experience of other trail users. If an area is posted "No Dogs," obey signage. This may mean that you leave your dog at home. It is also imperative that you exercise Leave No Trace practices with respect to removing any dog waste, packing out what your dog may leave on the trail. Be prepared with a plastic bag, and carry the waste until you come across a proper disposal receptacle.

6. **Don't Startle Other Trail Users:** A quick-moving trail runner, especially one who seemingly emerges from out of nowhere on an unsuspecting trail user, can be quite alarming. Give a courteous and audible announcement well in advance of your presence and intention to pass hikers on the trail, stating something like "On your left" or "Trail" as you approach the trail users. Keep in mind your announcement doesn't work well for those who are wearing headphones and blasting music. Show respect when passing by slowing down or stopping if necessary to prevent accidental contact. Be ready to yield to all other trail users (bikers, hikers, horses) even if you have the posted right of way. Uphill runners yield to downhill runners in most situations.

7. **Be Friendly:** The next step after not startling fellow users is letting them know they have a friend on the trail. Friendly communication is the key when trail users are yielding to one another. A "Thank you"

is fitting when others on the trail yield to you. A courteous "Hello, how are you?" shows kindness, which is particularly welcome.

8. **Don't Litter:** Pack out at least as much as you pack in. Gel wrappers with their little torn-off tops and old water bottles don't have a place on the trail. Consider wearing apparel with pockets that zip or a hydration pack that has a place to secure litter you find on the trail. Learn and use minimum impact techniques to dispose of human waste.

9. **Run in Small Groups:** Split larger groups into smaller groups. Larger groups can be very intimidating to hikers and have a greater environmental impact on trails. Most trail systems, parks, and wilderness areas have limits on group size. Familiarize yourself with the controlling policy and honor it.

10. **Safety:** Know the area you plan to run in, and let at least one other person know where you are planning to run and when you expect to return. Run with a buddy if possible. Take a map with you in unfamiliar areas. Be prepared for the weather and conditions prevailing when you start your run, and plan for the worst, given the likely duration of your run. Carry plenty of water, electrolyte replacement drink, or snacks for longer runs. Rescue efforts can be treacherous in remote areas. ATRA does not advise the use of headphones or iPods. The wearer typically hears nothing around them, including approaching wildlife and other humans. The most important safety aspect is to know and respect your limits. Report unusually dangerous, unsafe, or damaging conditions and activities to the proper authorities.

11. **Leave What You Find:** Leave natural or historic objects as you find them. This includes wildflowers and native grasses. Removing or collecting trail markers is serious vandalism that puts others at risk.

12. **Giving Back:** Volunteer, support, and encourage others to participate in trail maintenance days.

TRAIL RACE ETIQUETTE FOR THE RACE DIRECTION AND COMPETITOR

A few runners simply running on a trail normally have limited negative impacts. All the associated happenings of a trail race "event" add up and contribute to the total impact.

PREPARING FOR THE RACE AND SELECTING A COURSE

1. Involve the community. Make sure you secure all permits, permissions, and insurance. Cooperation from government officials (which

may include parks departments, USDA Forest Service, etc.) is a must. Be mindful of potential trail conflicts with other users, which may include hikers, bikers, equestrians, or hunters. Let other public trail and area users know of your event in advance by using the media, postings at trailheads, etc., so that they have a chance to avoid the area during your race and are not surprised by the presence of runners on race day.

2. Select a race course that uses officially designated open public trails. Trail runners may want to test the course before and after the event. Using existing trails has another benefit: The trail bed should be well-established, durable, and firm. If you are using private trails or going through areas that are normally off limits, let runners know this in advance, and strongly discourage them from using the route except on race day. Encourage your race participants to familiarize themselves with the race route only as much as is minimally necessary. Many popular race trails get "loved to death" during training by runners.

3. If existing trails don't offer the mileage or distance you would like to have as part of your course or the type of elevation gains or losses you need, adjust your race distance to accommodate what already exists. ATRA suggests you always use existing trails rather than creating social trails or detours.

4. Think about spectator, crew, and media movement around the course. This can often cause more damage than actual racing. Post signs to direct spectators to other course sections via established paths.

5. Limit the total number of participants allowed in your event in advance. Do not be greedy and blindly accept the number of entrants you might get. Work with land managing agencies to set a number that you, your staff, and the surrounding environment, trails, and facilities can safely accommodate with limited impact. Strive for quality of runner experience first and quantity of runners later only if increased numbers can be accepted comfortably.

6. Consider encouraging carpooling to your race by allocating preferential parking areas to vehicles with three or more runners, giving cash "gas money" incentives to those runners that carpool, etc.

7. Realize that most people visiting a natural area where your trail race will be held are visiting that area primarily to experience natural sights, sounds, and smells. Most trail race participants value these experiences also. Carefully consider how any "additions" to your event will impact and modify the natural experience for your race participants and others. Do you really need amplified music at the

start, finish, and aid stations? Will everyone appreciate cheering spectators? Are banners and mileage markers necessary? Can one course official silently standing at an intersection pointing the way take the place of numerous flagging and ground markings?

8. Consider the timing of your event so as not to conflict with other trail and area users during already heavily used time periods. Scheduling your event in the off-season may avoid potential conflicts.

9. Plan and position your aid stations to minimize conflicts with other users and to avoid environmental impacts. Locate them in areas where access is easy, durable, or previously disturbed surfaces already exist, and away from areas favored by other users (campgrounds, fishing spots, picnic areas, etc.).

10. Plan your start/finish area with care. Is there adequate parking? Will heavy concentrated use damage the vegetation or land? Do restrooms already exist or can they be brought in and removed easily? Is there a wide enough trail (or better yet a road) for the first part of the race to allow the field to spread out and runners to pass before they separate enough to allow safe use of a singletrack trail?

11. If trail or start/finish/aid area conditions cannot accommodate your race without environmental damage (due to mud, high water, downed trees, etc.), consider canceling, rescheduling, or having an alternative route in place for your event.

12. Encourage electronic registration. Post your event entry forms online instead of printing and distributing thousands, or at least print entry forms on recycled paper.

DURING THE RACE

1. Mark the course with ecofriendly markings. These markings may include flour or cake mix (devil's food is great for courses run on snow), colored construction marking tape, paper plates hung on trees with directional arrows, flagging. Remove all markings immediately following the race, but be sure your markers are still in place at race time so runners do not go off course.

2. Provide a large course map at the start/registration area so runners can familiarize themselves with the trail.

3. Don't allow participants to run with their dogs on the course. This is a safety issue for other participants and for the dogs. Dogs also have been known to tow runners to an unfair advantage in a race.

4. Use the race as an opportunity to educate runners and spectators about responsible trail running. Include information about responsible

training and volunteerism in each racer's entry packet. If you have a race announcer, provide him or her with a variety of short public messages that talk about responsible use of trails, joining a trail running club, and volunteering to maintain trails.

5. Encourage local trail advocacy organizations to share their information with the public at your event. If the race includes a product expo, allow local advocacy groups to exhibit without charge.

6. Green the event. Provide adequate portable toilets, drinking water, and trash receptacles. Let runners know where these will be located in advance. Recycle all cans, bottles, paper, and glass. Consider recyclable materials for awards and organic T-shirts for participants. Event organizers and all participants will benefit if they are seen as being at the forefront of energy and materials conservation. As a participant, carry a water bottle and refill at the aid station so you are not using extra cups. As a race director, consider *requiring* participants to start the race with their own fluid and food in a container (water bottle or pack) so as to eliminate the need for cups along the trail. Pack out your gel wrappers and trash. You as the participant should be responsible for your trash.

7. Limit spectator and crew access to points along the course that can safely accommodate them and their vehicles without damage. Consider prohibiting all spectator and crew access to the trail to preserve the trail experience for the participants and to limit impacts.

8. Promote local recreational trail running by making sure that maps, guidebooks, and brochures are available at the race. Involve local schoolchildren in the event in a kids' run if you have the resources.

9. Stop to help others in need, even while racing, and sacrifice your own event to aid other trail users who might be in trouble.

10. ATRA suggests participants refrain from using iPods/headphones in races. This is foremost a safety issue. Many running insurance providers do not permit use of these devices.

11. When you have two-way traffic, slower runners yield to faster runners, and on ascent/descents, the uphill runner should yield to the downhill runner.

12. Try to be patient when you are part of a conga line on crowded racing trails. Instead of creating social trails by passing a runner above or below the marked trail, yell out, "Trail" and "To your left" or "To your right." If you are the slower runner, stop and step aside to make it easier for the faster runner to overtake you.

13. ATRA does not condone bandit runners (unregistered runners). Not only are bandits a serious safety and liability concern for the race director, often there are limits in races set forth by a permit. Bandits can jeopardize the issuance of future permits.
14. Require runners to follow all race rules, including staying on the designated marked route, packing out everything they started the race with, not having crew/pacers/spectators on the route, etc. Send a strong statement by disqualifying those runners who do not follow the rules.

AFTER THE RACE
1. Do a thorough job of cleaning the start-finish area, parking lots, and repairing and restoring the trails used for the event. Leave the trails in better shape than they were in prior to the race. Document your restoration work with photos.
2. If your event has been financially successful, make a contribution to your local trail-running advocacy group and, if possible, to ATRA, too. When you do this, send press releases announcing your donations. This will enhance your image in the local community.
3. Get a capable runner to run sweep of your entire race route as soon as possible after the event. This runner can pick up trash, course markings, note any trail damage that needs to be mitigated, gauge reaction from other trail users they encounter, as well as act as a safety net. This runner should carry a pack, cell phone, first aid kit, etc.

APPENDIX B: ROAD RUNNERS CLUB OF AMERICA GENERAL RUNNING SAFETY TIPS

- **Don't wear headphones**. Use your ears to be aware of your surroundings. Your ears may help you avoid dangers your eyes may miss during evening or early morning runs.
- **Run against traffic so you can observe approaching automobiles.** By facing oncoming traffic, you may be able to react quicker than if it is behind you.
- **Look both ways before crossing.** Be sure the driver of a car acknowledges your right-of-way before crossing in front of a vehicle. Obey traffic signals.
- **Carry identification or write your name, phone number, and blood type on the inside sole of your running shoe.** Include any important medical information.
- **Always stay alert and aware of what's going on around you.** The more aware you are, the less vulnerable you are.
- **Carry a cell phone or change for a phone call.** Know the locations of public phones along your regular route.
- **Trust your intuition about a person or an area.** React on your intuition and avoid a person or situation if you're unsure. If something tells you a situation is not "right," it isn't.
- **Alter or vary your running route pattern; run in familiar areas if possible.** In unfamiliar areas, such as while traveling, contact a local chapter of Road Runners Club of America or a local running store. Know where open businesses or stores are located in case of emergency.
- **Run with a partner.** Run with a dog.
- **Write down or leave word of the direction of your run.** Tell friends and family of your favorite running routes.
- **Avoid unpopulated areas, deserted streets, and overgrown trails.** Avoid unlit areas, especially at night. Run clear of parked cars or bushes.
- **Ignore verbal harassment and do not verbally harass others.** Use discretion in acknowledging strangers. Look directly at others and be observant, but keep your distance and keep moving.
- **Wear reflective material if you must run before dawn or after dark.** Avoid running on the street when it is dark.
- **Practice memorizing license tags or identifying characteristics of strangers.**

- **Carry a noisemaker.** Get training in self-defense.
- **When using multiuse trails, follow the rules of the road.** If you alter your direction, look over your shoulder before crossing the trail to avoid a potential collision with an oncoming cyclist or passing runner.
- **Call police immediately if something happens to you or someone else or you notice anyone out of the ordinary.** It is important to report incidents immediately.

APPENDIX C: USEFUL WEBSITES

- www.trailrunner.com
- www.trailrunproject.com
- www.strava.com
- www.trailsandopenspaces.org
- Northwest Trail Runs: http://nwtrailruns.com
- Evergreen Trail Races: http://evergreentrailruns.com/
- Rainshadow Running (specifically Deception Pass race: http://www.rainshadowrunning.com/deception-pass-25k.html)
- Running Stoes: The Balanced Athlete - https://www.facebook.com/thebalancedathlete (located in Renton)
- Seven Hills Running Shop: http://sevenhillsrunningshop.com/
- Super Jock 'n Jill LLC: https://superjocknjill.com/
- Seattle Running Club: http://www.seattlerunningclub.org
- Seattle Running Meetups: https://www.meetup.com/topics/trail-running/us/wa/seattle/